MYTHOLOGY PUZZLES

MYTHOLOGY
PUZZLES

PUZZLES INSPIRED BY CLASSICAL GREEK
& ROMAN MYTHS AND LEGENDS

JOEL JESSUP

SIRIUS

Picture Credits:

Wellcome Collection: Pages 149, 202, and 208
Met Museum, Gift of Harry G. Friedman, 1961: Page 213

SIRIUS

This edition published in 2024 by Sirius Publishing, a division of
Arcturus Publishing Limited,
26/27 Bickels Yard, 151–153 Bermondsey Street,
London SE1 3HA

ISBN: 978-1-3988-3694-5
AD011151NT

Printed in China

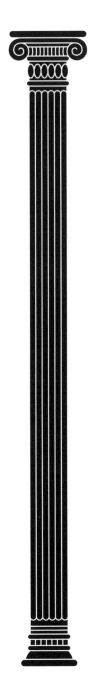

CONTENTS

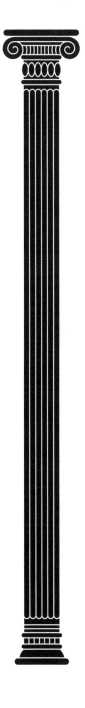

INTRODUCTION

Hercules. The Trojan Horse. The Odyssey. Medusa. The Amazons.
Classical mythology, also known as Greco-Roman
Mythology, is a big part of modern culture. Why, the very
planets of our solar system are named after the Roman Gods!
Countless businesses and fashion brands bear the name of
classical Gods and heroes. And what are modern superhero
stories if not retellings of some of these incredible tales?

The vast quantity of myths and legends that originate from
Ancient Greek and Roman culture are stories bursting with
passion, intrigue, mystery, and adventure.

These tales have come to us through different means.
Originally the stories and legends would survive in oral histories
and retellings, and in the everyday culture of the

civilization in question, whether visiting a temple or
holding a festival. Mosaics, statues, and decorated
vases and urns would depict them. Then
manuscripts, and later printed documents, would
preserve these stories in physical text.

But the origin and true nature of some of these tales is sometimes mysterious, despite the sheer volume of study. Myth was recorded as history or as legend, changing as time went on. Even the authors of these works were possibly legendary and mythical, like the poet Homer.

When the Romans adopted the Greek Gods as their own and mixed them with their own legends and stories, this muddied the waters of time further, especially as the Roman way of life and worship was not the same as that of Greece.

Presented here for the first time is a retelling of some of the most compelling stories in Greco-Roman mythology, in the form of a series of mysterious puzzles. In the spirit of the centuries of reinvention that the myths have already faced, these stories have been changed, remixed, and reinterpreted, and so details from them may differ from the traditional telling.

However they are told, the core power of classical myths endures, and as you read this book you will find in them something new or exciting you never knew before!

TROJAN HORSE

After a 10-year siege of the city of Troy, the Greek army, led by Odysseus, devised a clever plan: they would build a wooden horse and pretend to leave, suggesting it had been left as a gift for their "victorious" foes (the horse being the symbol of the city). However, inside the horse would be hidden 50 of Greece's greatest warriors, including Odysseus himself. Once the horse was brought into the city, the warriors would emerge and attack the city from within, conquering Troy! The horse would be 12 podes wide, 31 podes tall, and 18 podes long.

[NB: Podes is the plural of *pous,* a Greek unit of measurement as long as the average Greek sandal (size 10).]

However, there was a major problem with the construction of the horse: its chief builder, Epeius, did not have enough materials to make one that would allow 50 soldiers to be inside; he could only build one that had room for 40 soldiers. This smaller horse was, however, still effective, and the Greeks' plan worked, and became legend.

 Question: What are the dimensions of the 40-man horse they built (width, height and length) in feet?

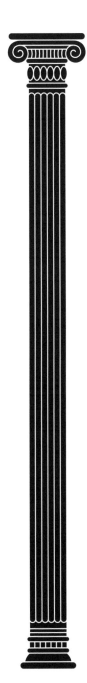

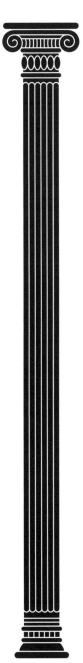

Escaping the Labyrinth

In the legend that we all know, every year 14 young nobles would be sent into the labyrinth at Knossos to be consumed by the Minotaur, the monstrous half-man, half-bull created by Minos and Poseidon's actions. Theseus joined the group with the intention of slaying the Minotaur and ending the sacrifices. The king's daughter Ariadne had fallen in love with Theseus and given him a ball of thread with which to retrace his path and leave the maze.

> *"Take care of this," she said, placing it in his left hand.*
> *"Without it you may find what you think is the right way is wrong."*

As they entered the labyrinth, Theseus fixed the thread to the entrance.

But what is unknown is that after Theseus slew the Minotaur in a great battle, he found that the string had become waterlogged and rotten, destroyed by Poseidon himself in a rage at Theseus' arrogance.

The weary Theseus leaned on the wall of the labyrinth, peering forward at the impossible path that lay ahead.

> *"So many walls to pass," one of the youths muttered, feeling defeated.*
> *"There is but one wall, really," said another, "winding around itself."*

Theseus looked at his hand on the wall, then at the labyrinth, and ... he knew how to get them out. It would take a long time, but it was guaranteed to work.

 Question: What is the guaranteed way for Theseus to lead them out of the labyrinth?

PERSEUS AND THE HESPERIDES

Perseus had foolishly promised Polydectes any gift he desired, and it was the head of Medusa that Polydectes demanded! But even if he managed to take her head, he could not carry it safely.

Luckily, he tricked the Graeae into telling him the location of the Hesperides, the beautiful maidens who tended to Hera's orchard. They had a magical knapsack called a *kibisis,* which could bear any object, even Medusa's head.

When he arrived at the garden he found seven women, rather than the three he expected. They said their names were Aiopis, Antheia, Donakis, Calypso, Mermesa, Nelisa and Tara – but they didn't say who was who!

"If you want the kibisis, you must discover our names!" they laughed, standing in a line, 1 to 7. The girl at number 6 has it, but who is she?

We will give you the following clues:

- Mermesa is number 2.
- The person to the left of Nelisa has a name beginning with A.
- The person to the right of Nelisa has 4 letters in their name.
- Donakis is 4 to the left of Tara.
- The woman at number 3 has a name ending with S.
- Antheia is at an odd number!

 Question: In what order are they standing, and who has the knapsack?

PANDORA'S JAR

Knowledge of Pandora's box – the magical artefact that, when opened, released things like cruelty and illness into the world – is so universal that the name itself has become synonymous with the idea of unintentionally releasing some threat to humanity to disrupt its harmony. But the details of the myth itself, like many classical myths, differ based on who is telling it.

Interestingly, the artefact was actually a jar. In the original myth, Zeus, the father of the gods, was driven nearly to madness by the perceived injustice of Prometheus taking fire from the gods. And, after ensuring the security of Olympus, Zeus commanded that Hephaestus create Pandora, the first woman. They then sent her bearing the jar to Epimetheus, Prometheus' brother, in a supposed "olive branch" of peace.

In the 17th century, in his Latin translation, Erasmus replaced *pithos* (jar) with *pyxis* (box) – so, in all fairness, scholars have the freedom to use either term without being accused of ignorance.

The second thing is that not every version of the story says the jar was full of evils and designed to cause sadness. There is some conflict between accounts, because in some retellings, the jar contained all the good things of the world, her gift to them as an act of mercy for the future health of humankind.

In most retellings, one thing remained in the jar: hope. Whether this is a source of joy or a harbinger of discord also differs. Trying to square all the different versions with each other has tested many scholars' sanity. But rather than despair at this, most realize that the numerous differences show the changing perception of morality through time.

Question: In this text, there are 10 vices and 11 virtues. Find them all and match them with their opposites, revealing the unmatched virtue that remained in the jar.

DIP STYX

Another phrase from Greek mythology that everyone uses is "Achilles' heel," meaning a singular weakness that can be exploited.

Achilles was a legendary Greek hero and formidable fighter, famed for his activities in the Trojan war. His talents were often attributed to the fact that when he was a baby his mother bathed him in the river Styx in a bid to grant him immortality. But she had to hold him by his heel to do so, and that part of his body was never submerged, leaving it vulnerable to attack; ultimately, he was killed by an arrow hitting his heel in battle.

Less well known are the other Greek heroes who were dipped into the Styx by their parents or guardians! This is because their deaths were much less heroic.

Achaeus bled out after receiving a paper cut from a particularly sharp piece of papyrus when he was beginning to write his memoirs. For that reason, we do not know what he did, but we have a sample of his blood and a fingerprint.

Bienor was killed by the terrible wailing lament that his parents had arranged for his leaving party. He therefore never made it to the Trojan war at all.

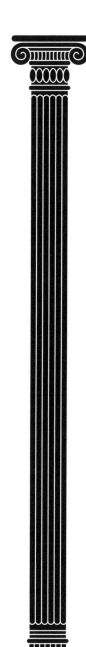

Caucon was undone by vanity, as the olive oil he used to condition his hair after washing it had been poisoned by a rival.

Demodice, surprisingly, died during a particularly strenuous version of an ancient Greek ballgame. Its name is lost to time, but in many ways, it resembles the modern game of tennis.

Epicasta is the strangest, as she fought an entire horde of Harpies to a standstill; but when she dropped her shield and knelt to pick it up, she perished immediately.

 Question: Which body parts were each of these heroes held by when they were dipped into the Styx?

CIRCE'S CURSES

During the Odyssey, Odysseus' one remaining ship – its crew tired and partially bitten – came to a mysterious wooded island called Aeaea. At its middle was a strange stone house occupied by a beautiful, friendly goddess named Circe.

But Odysseus and his men did not realize that Circe was also an enchantress who had the power to transform men into animals. She served Odysseus' men a specially prepared mess of cheese, honey, meal and Pramnian wine, which they ate hungrily, only to find themselves transforming into swine! Ultimately, with the assistance of Hermes, Odysseus himself was able to avoid transformation, and Circe took pity on them and returned them to human form.

They remained there for a year, and during this time Odysseus saw many other oddly sized animals on the island: a snail crawling across a pile of gold. A magpie darting around with incredible speed. A gentle deer, cowering from predators. A wolf pack in which one of the wolves had a strangely glittering coat. A muddy brown tortoise he briefly mistook for a rock. And a huge fish in the crystal-clear water of her fountain.

"Are they…men?" Odysseus asked Circe.

"They were, yes," Circe said. "Each of them came here for something they thought they wanted. And instead, I gave them what they needed.

A drunkard came here, a disciple of Dionysus, because he had sworn to drink only wine and heard the finest vintage lay in my cellar.

A hermit came here to isolate himself from society. On my island!

An idle man came because he had heard there were maidens here who would wait on him hand and foot.

A thief came here to steal the treasures he had heard I had gathered, as did a pirate, looking for more jewels and gaudy trinkets to add to his bright outfit.

And a man came to murder me on behalf of his patron, the goddess Artemis."

 Question: Can you guess which man became which animal?

Hercules' First Labour:
The Nemean Lion

Hercules (originally known by his Greek name, Heracles) was a legendary figure, a son of Zeus and an indomitable hero.

The famous 12 labours were undertaken by Hercules to atone for a terrible, violent act he committed under the influence of his worst enemy: Hera, Zeus' wife. He was told by Pythia, the oracle of Delphi, to go and serve King Eurystheus for 10 years as a way of atoning, little knowing that Eurystheus served Hera. The labours that Eurystheus assigned him were designed to be impossible, or incredibly dangerous, in the hope that Hercules would die or be tarnished.

His first challenge was to slay an unkillable lion, which had been prowling around the hills surrounding the town of Nemea. No-one had been able to defeat it, and when Hercules first engaged it in battle he learned why: The arrows he fired simply snapped as they struck the Nemean lion's impenetrable golden skin! He tried again with spear and sword, but nothing could penetrate its fur, and when it slashed him with its razor-sharp claws, the enormous, bloody lacerations it left proved that Hercules' skin was nowhere near as tough as the lion's.

Its strength, while not quite the match of Hercules, was formidable, and he had to dodge blow after blow; the lion even smashed a tree to splinters with its huge paws! Some versions of the story claim that he bested it by firing an arrow into its mouth, but its enormous teeth were more than capable of biting any arrow in two long before it could damage anything within its throat.

Hercules, bloodied and exhausted, knew he could not beat it in hand-to-hand combat, and could not penetrate its fur. The lion, too, was tired, and retreated to its lair. Seeing his advantage, Hercules followed stealthily, but even his bravery shrank when he saw that lying at the mouth of the cave was the slashed body of another lion! Its fur was just as golden and impenetrable as that of their kin, so the lion he fought was not just mighty, but mighty enough to kill its chief rival.

And yet it gave him an idea. He approached the body, took something from it, and was able to not only kill the Nemean lion, but skin it and wear its pelt!

 Question: How did Hercules kill and then skin the Nemean lion?

THE SECOND LABOUR:
THE LERNAEAN HYDRA

For his second labour, the king tells Hercules to defeat the Hydra, a gigantic water serpent that dwells in the lake of Lerna.

"She is the child of Typhon and Echidna, but her power and hideousness outweigh even theirs. Her breath is poisonous and her blood too, and even if you smell it, you will die. It has three mighty heads, with blazing eyes as big as shields and jagged, sharp teeth like dorata," the king said. "Well...good luck."

Hercules marched off boldly, rebuffing the king's attempts to scare him. But what the king had not told him was that whenever one of the Hydra's heads was severed from its neck, the neck would split in twain and grow into two new heads!

Athena, goddess of wisdom, sought out Hercules' nephew Iolaus and told him of this.

"Once the head is severed, it takes as long to grow back as it does for Hercules to sever it. But if you cauterize the stump with a firebrand, it will not grow back. It should take you 29 seconds to do this. Go to him!"

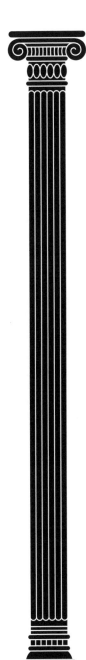

Iolaus ran to the lake and as he arrived, he saw that Hercules had already severed a head and was in the act of severing a second. The first head had not grown back yet, and Hercules greeted his nephew cheerily.

> "Well met, Iolaus! I am halfway through this beast's second neck..." he shouted, as Iolaus immediately began cauterizing the first stump.
> "HOW LONG DID THE FIRST TAKE YOU?!" Iolaus shouted, holding his nose against the poisonous fumes.
> "I don't recall. But halfway took me 15 seconds."
> "Ah."

 Question: How many heads will Hercules have to sever before the beast is defeated?

THE THIRD LABOUR:
THE CERYNEIAN HIND

After these two shows of might, Eurystheus decided the next labour should be a test of Hercules' speed.

In Ceryneia there was an enormous hind, a female deer that nonetheless had huge golden antlers and bronze hooves, and snorted fire. It was the fastest land animal in the world. Hercules had to capture it, but he wanted to do so without harming it because it was beloved of Artemis, goddess of the hunt, and she would exact a fierce revenge on him unless he showed her due consideration.

Hercules was very swift of foot, and chased the hind for an entire year. But ultimately he concluded that he would have to wound the beast if he were to have any chance of stopping it. He knew that the hind was capable of running twice the speed of any normal arrow, but he had been gifted a silver bow by Apollo, and he knew that any arrow fired from it would initially travel at the average speed of an arrow (300km an hour), but then would increase in speed by 1km a second every minute.

 Question: What is the speed of the hind; and if Hercules fires an arrow from this bow at the hind from 10km away, and there is no obstruction or other adverse effect from wind or anything else, can it strike the hind?

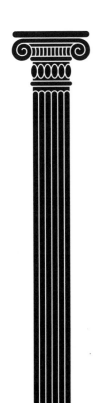

THE FOURTH LABOUR:
THE ERYMANTHIAN BOAR

Eurystheus grew increasingly furious at Hercules' success. Then he learned about a boar that lived on Mount Erymanthos that generated a great fear in any who saw it – even the famously staunch Centaur tribe that lived there. He gave Hercules the task of capturing it alive, in the hope that he, too, would be too cowardly to succeed.

After an unfortunate encounter with the Centaurs, Hercules finally came to the boar's territory at around dawn. Unlike the hind, the boar was hated by Artemis, but she had been forbidden to hunt it by her twin brother, Apollo (who rode the sun chariot), as he claimed it as his own personal quarry.

When Hercules spotted the boar in the distance to the north, he did not find it frightening to look upon. In fact, maybe the boar was afraid of him, as it quickly began running to Hercules' left! He gave chase and followed the boar as it ran west. Surprisingly, the boar was very fast, and for hours Hercules chased the boar as its path changed from running west to north, and then finally running east! Hercules caught up to the boar just as the sun had finally set... only for it to immediately turn around and snarl directly into Hercules' face with incredible ferocity before goring him with its tusks! As Hercules retreated in the dark, he reasoned that it must not have been him that the boar was running from. Suddenly Hercules laughed as he realized the truth of the matter,, and with that information was able to corner the boar in a snowbank.

 Question: What was the boar running from?

25

The Fifth Labour:
Augean Stables

The judge peered cynically at Hercules as he stood in the witness box of the court of King Augeas.

"And you say that you cleaned out the Augean stables single-handedly?"
"That's correct," said Hercules boldly. "The cattle were each producing 30 kilograms of manure a day. For 30 years! No-one had cleaned it, and yet I did it in a day. That's a great achievement if you ask me! And the king promised me 300 of the cattle in return."
"His majesty's offer of 10% of the cattle is not the source of this dispute, Mr. Hercules," said the judge. "And what is a kilogram?"
"We're using metric measurements today, Judge," said his clerk. "It's a modern translation for the purposes of a puzzle. We're also using the Roman calendar."
"Ah, yes, discounting leap years, I hope," the judge said, examining his papyrus. "Nevertheless, the reason we are here is that his regal majesty, lord of all he surveys, accurately observed that it was not you who cleaned out the stables."
Hercules scoffed at this. "I rerouted two entire rivers so that they would flow through the stables! I dug giant trenches from the rivers to the stable, so that they would wash away the enormous quantities of manure! No-one helped."

"This is true... but does that not mean the rivers themselves were the ones that cleaned out the stables?" asked the judge with an air of satisfaction.

"If you sweep a courtyard clean, is it you who gets the credit, or the broom?" asked Hercules, visibly tiring of this debacle.

"But the 'courtyard' isn't clean, Mr. Hercules. You flushed over a billion 'kilograms' of cow dung across the entire kingdom!" said the judge, who had been in his garden at the time.

"Before I washed it away, the mound of manure was bigger than Mount Olympus!" replied Hercules.

The judge considered this, then was handed a piece of paper by the clerk.

"Ah, I see the king has decided to just banish you from the country anyway. And have me executed. Shame."

"Sorry, sir," said Hercules. "I suppose I'll just kill him and install his son on the throne instead. I've had enough of this."

 Question: How much cow dung was at the stables when Hercules arrived to clean them?

THE SIXTH LABOUR:
DEFEAT THE
STYMPHALIAN BIRDS

Enraged at Hercules' smug success, Eurystheus decided to use Hercules' incredible strength against him. At this point Eurystheus had taken to hiding in a large *pithos*, a storage jar that dwelt in his basement, because he had been so frightened by the lion and the boar. Hercules descended to the basement and at first could not hear what Eurystheus was saying, until his attendant opened the lid.

> *"... irds."*
> *"What?"*
> *"I said, you must journey to Lake Stymphalia and kill the dreaded birds!" Eurystheus shouted, and Hercules noted that the hollow aperture of the jar actually amplified the king's normally weak voice.*
> *"A bunch of birds? No problem."*

Hercules thought this labour was much easier than killing an indestructible lion or a regenerating sea snake, even though he had heard the Stymphalian birds had bronze beaks and metal feathers they could fire like arrows. The birds had been attacking and destroying the local area in huge flocks.

However, when he arrived, it seemed the birds had anticipated his arrival and retreated to the now swamp-like lake area.

28

As he entered this zone, he suddenly found his feet sinking into the mire, his legendary muscular bulk pulling him down!

This was a conundrum. He left the area, and the birds resumed their attacks; but no matter how he tried to sneak back, they would immediately retreat to the swamp.

Feeling defeated, he was surprised to see the figure of Athena, goddess of wisdom, appear before him bearing some kind of castanet or rattle.

"This krotala *was built by Hephaestus to aid you. His legendary skills of manufacture have ensured its noise will agitate and frighten the birds into flight."*

Bearing the krotala, Hercules climbed a nearby mountain, pausing only to refresh himself in a small lake near the peak. When at the optimum point, he began using the krotala, and it produced a loud, rhythmic clacking sound, like none he had ever heard.

And yet it was not loud enough to reach the ears of the birds in the swamp. He needed to enhance the sound somewhat. Thinking quickly, Hercules remembered something he had done just before he had come to this spot, and also how he had solved the fifth labour. Soon he had a place to stand where the sound was loud enough, and as the birds flew into the air, he slaughtered most of them, shooting them out of the air with arrows poisoned with the Hydra's blood!

 Question: How did Hercules amplify the sound of the krotala?

THE SEVENTH LABOUR: CAPTURE THE CRETAN BULL

Eurystheus, angry and feeling cramped in his jar, decided to try and get the other gods to become angered toward Hercules, so he instructed Hercules to capture the famous Cretan bull. This legendary creature had been presented to King Minos by Poseidon so he could sacrifice it to the sea god. But Minos liked the bull so much he let it live, and Poseidon's rage led – through a series of escalating circumstances – to Minos' wife Pasiphaë giving birth to Asterion, the half-human, half-bull Minotaur.

Unsurprisingly, when he arrived at Knossos, King Minos was quite happy for Hercules to remove the bull from the kingdom. And the actual capture of the bull was also much easier than that of the hind or the boar, as it was not supernaturally strong or fast, just very charismatic. Hercules snuck up behind it and got it in a chokehold, releasing it once it was unconscious, and shipped it back to Eurystheus, who didn't know what to do with it!

He proposed sacrificing it to Hera, but she felt that Hercules would get reflected glory from this act, and ultimately the bull was once again released! It wandered to a place where, many years later, a great battle would take place. Philippides, a mere messenger, would undertake an act that would cement the name of this place in history, not because of its people or its culture but simply because of its distance from Athens. It was part of a famous series of sporting events almost two millennia later, and was in fact also based on a place supposedly founded by Hercules, just after he had cleared out the stables.

Question:
To which place
did the bull wander?

THE EIGHTH LABOUR:
THE MARES OF DIOMEDES

"Hercules can transport a wild beast on its own... but can he transport the four wildest horses in the land?"

Eurystheus roared to himself in his pythia. He sent a servant to Hercules with a demand: "Bring him the mares of Diomedes!"

Hercules had heard tell of the monstrous beasts, kept as pets by King Diomedes and fed primarily on the flesh of anyone unfortunate enough to be captured by – or stumble upon the land of – the Bistones, Diomedes' tribe.

Hercules considered taking a full complement of men, but was wary of the thought that it would mean he would not take sole credit for the labour. Instead he went alone, and made a big show of visiting the court of King Diomedes, feigning ignorance of the mares and their true nature. He made a big show of getting drunk, but as everyone joined in and then shortly after passed out, he snuck off, carrying the unconscious form of the king himself.

The giant mares were tethered by iron chains to a huge bronze trough, so mighty was their strength. One had a bright yellow mane and skin, and was sleeping on the ground. A second had strangely shining fur, like gold, and was licking at the empty trough with its back to Hercules. A third was leaning up against a tree, the chain pulled as taut as possible, its eyes closed in slumber. And a fourth stood staring directly at him, its eyes almost burning with rage.

He knew their names: Deinos. Xanthos. Lampon. Podargos. And he'd overheard that of that group only Podargos (the swift) had not eaten recently. When their bellies were full, the mares were pliable; but he had to ensure that the fourth horse had a fine meal…that of the tyrannical king they served. But which horse was which? The only other things he knew were that Lampon was not asleep; Xanthos had a yellowish hue of some kind (or was it gold?); Athena had whispered to him that neither Lampon nor Podargos could see him; and Deinos was standing up.

 Question: Which horse is Podargos?

The Ninth Labour:
The Belt of Hippolyta

For his ninth labour, Eurystheus sent Hercules to claim the belt of Hippolyta, the leader of the warlike Amazons, an all-female tribe of hunters who dwelled on the island of Themiscyra. Eurystheus claimed he wanted it for his daughter Admete, but in truth he and Hera hoped that Hercules would immediately be rejected by them.

Hercules decided to take a retinue of men and set off on an ocean journey; but he accidentally ended up on the island of Panos, which was inhabited only by the sons of King Minos: Eurymedon, Chryses, Nephalion and Philolaus.

They took against him, and in their attack killed a third of the men who had sailed with Hercules. Hercules in turn killed half of their own forces. Then his remaining men besieged the group until they agreed to replace those that they had killed. As the crew departed, this left the island uninhabited.

 Question: How many men left on the journey, and how many arrived in Themiscyra, including Hercules?

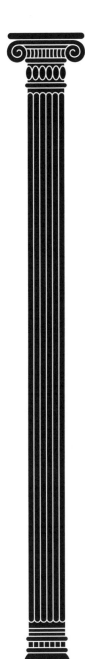

THE TENTH LABOUR:
THE CATTLE OF GERYON

"This ninth labour was most dismaying," Hercules said
as he handed Eurystheus' servant the belt.
"I met Hippolyta alone, and then thought she had set an
ambush; so I killed her and took the belt. But I realize now
that a dark force had turned the Amazons against me."

Eurystheus remained quiet, as he knew it was his goddess, Hera, that had done this. But annoyingly, Hercules had still completed the labour.

"Um…go get me the cattle of Geryon," he blurted out.
"The three-headed giant who lives at the very edge
of the world? How many of his cattle?"
"All. Bring them all here alive. Then you have completed your labours."

At this point, the events of Hercules' journey have become distorted by time, and the following events are not chronological. Can you discern their true order?

1. Hercules gives the cattle to Eurystheus, who sacrifices them to Hera.
2. The sun god Helios admires Hercules' bravery and gives him a magical golden cup.
3. Hercules gathers the scattered cattle and gets them across a river by filling it with rocks.
4. Hercules journeys through the Libyan desert. Enraged by the heat, he fires an arrow at the sun!
5. Hercules is able to travel across the sea in the golden cup.
6. Hercules fights the three-headed Geryon and is able to kill him with poisoned arrows.
7. Hera sends a gadfly, and the cattle disperse.
8. Upon arrival at the island of Erythia, Hercules is immediately attacked by Orthrus, the two-headed guard dog, which he slays.
9. Hercules puts the cattle into his goblet and sails them back across the sea.
10. Hercules returns the goblet to the sun and sets off with the cattle.

 Question: What's the correct order of these events?

The Eleventh Labour:
The Golden Apples of the Hesperides

Eurystheus told Hercules his labours were not over.

"You did not defeat the Hydra alone!" the king shouted from his jar. "And it was the rivers that cleaned the Augean stables, not thee! You must complete two more labours. Bring me…golden apples from the garden of the Hesperides!"

Hercules lured the Old Man of the Sea to the shore and trapped him, suspecting he knew where the legendary garden was. And he did: in the same place where Geryon lived!

"Eurystheus will never release you, Hercules," the Old Man of the Sea hissed. "He hates you. Everyone knows."

On his way back to the islands he saw the Titan Prometheus, chained to a rock and cursed to forever have his liver pecked out by an eagle. Hercules freed him with an arrow, and Prometheus told Hercules he couldn't take any golden apples from the garden, as it was guarded by an invincible dragon called Ladon. He suggested instead that Atlas, another Titan, could get the apples, as the Hesperides were his daughters.

Atlas was cursed to bear the entire sky on his shoulders as a punishment, and was exiled on a mist-shrouded island. Hercules travelled there and offered to bear the sky. Atlas would be permitted relief from his torment as long as he went to get the apples.

Atlas kept his word, and got them, but as he returned to Hercules, he suddenly realized he had an idea. He would return the apples himself to Eurystheus as a favour to Hercules…while Hercules continued to hold the sky.

This loophole would mean that Atlas could walk free and Hercules would bear the sky forever! Some tales say that Hercules tricked Atlas into taking the sky back by asking for a moment free of it to adjust his tunic, so the sky would sit better on his shoulders. But an earlier version of the legend has Hercules find a stranger solution. As Atlas prepared to leave, Hercules prayed to Athena and asked that she tell his men to sail toward this island bearing two lamps of Greek fire and using Hephaestus' *krotala*.

 Question: What does Hercules say to Atlas to make him take back the sky?
a. That holding the sky is actually very enjoyable.
b. That a huge monster is coming and that only he, Hercules, can defeat it.
c. That Eurystheus would only accept the apples from Hercules.

THE TWELFTH LABOUR:
CAPTURE CERBERUS

For the twelfth labour, Eurystheus sought a task impossible for even the mighty Hercules. So he commanded him to enter the Underworld – the kingdom of Hades, where mortals went to die – and bring back Cerberus, the giant, demonic, three-headed dog that guards its entrance.

First Hercules was initiated into the Eleusinian Mysteries; he learned the story of Persephone's abduction by Hades, and Demeter's desperate quest to secure her return from the Underworld.

> *"Young man, remember that this tale, like all, serves the purpose of its teller," said the priest mysteriously. "And if you find yourself doubting, there is nothing wrong with going back."*

Hercules took that to mean that he would be better off tackling Cerberus from behind than by facing it head on. Knowing that Cerberus guarded the Underworld's entrance at Tainaron, he instead travelled to an alternative entrance in Acherusia. This was usually used as an exit, so it was not as well known – or well guarded. Hercules then journeyed through the entire Underworld before arriving behind the monstrous hound. Only by using chains was he able to subdue and bind it.

Once he was finished, he looked up and saw that there were three identical sealed doorways.

Cerberus' middle head spoke.

"Three doors there are, and three heads have I. One door leads to escape, the other two to eternal imprisonment. Of my heads, one speaks the truth – except for questions about the Underworld. One speaks only lies – except for questions about the other heads. And one speaks the truth if the head that has spoken before it has lied, but speaks lies if the previous head has spoken the truth. You may ask only two questions."

Hercules turned to the first head.

"Which door leads to the surface?"
"The third door," the dog's first head uttered gruffly.

He turned to the third head.

"Does the first head speak truly?"
"No," the dog's third head intoned.

Hercules considered this and realized which exit he needed to use.

 Question: Which exit should Hercules use to leave the Underworld?

THE FALL OF ICARUS

After Theseus made his way through the labyrinth and killed the Minotaur, King Minos decided to imprison the maze's designer, Daedalus, as well as his son Icarus. He suspected them of telling Ariadne to give Theseus the thread, although Daedalus suspected he simply wanted someone to blame...

"This tower cannot be escaped," Minos growled. "The exit has been sealed and you are 200 feet up. I have included a window, though. I am not a monster."

What Minos did not consider was that he had imprisoned the greatest inventor of the age, and Daedalus began the construction of wings for both himself and his son, gathering the feathers of flocking birds and using beeswax to glue them to structures made from clothing and linen and wood.

Finally their wings were complete, but they needed to test them to ensure they would work.

On the first day, Daedalus was concerned about the dim daylight and choppy seas with occasional bursts of wind. But they managed to glide from the tower and then circle back with little effort, even if the humidity led to some of the feathers becoming unstuck.

Icarus was excited to go out on the second day, as he had found the flight exhilarating. The humidity had reduced, and although the daylight was still dim, there were hints of light in the distance. Birds were flying higher in the sky, so they had to dodge them somewhat. But they found they could fly even further than before, and they returned to rest for the next day, and their hopeful escape.

On the last day, all the signs seemed to be on their side. The birds were flying higher than ever. Visibility was much better, depending on the angle at which you were flying. It was warmer but less humid. The sky was blue.

I think many of us know what happened next. Icarus flew too close to the sun and his wings disintegrated, while his father survived. But there was another factor that made the first two days more successful than the last.

 Question: What was it that ensured that Icarus survived the two days of tests they made, but died on the third?

THE QUEST OF PERSEUS

Four generations earlier lived another of Zeus' children: Hercules' ancestor Perseus. As a child he was thrown into a wooden crate, along with his mother, Danaë, by her father, King Acrisius. Acrisius was fearful of a prophecy that said his grandson would kill him, but was too afraid of Zeus' retribution to execute either of them, so he had the crate tossed into the ocean. They ended up on an island, where they were hauled out by Dictys the fisherman, and ended up joining the court of his brother, King Polydectes. It is here that Perseus' adventures began...

PERSEUS PART I: BYOH

As Perseus grew up, he could not fail to notice King Polydectes' interest in his mother and, as she did not share this interest, he would protect her. The scheming Polydectes therefore sought to get rid of Perseus, either through disgrace or death.

He decided to do this in the most obvious way: He threw a "bring your own horse" party, knowing that Perseus didn't have one and would therefore be unintentionally insulting his host. The party was in honour of Hippodamia, and to drive home his point Polydectes told the story of the famous legend about her suitors:

"King Oenomaus had been told a prophecy that he would be killed by his son-in-law. A lot of that going around in those days! So he declared that any man who sought to be her suitor had to defeat him in a chariot race. And he was excellent at chariot racing. He successfully defeated and executed 18 of her

suitors and used to decorate the spires of his palace with their severed heads. Pelops wanted to marry Hippodamia and had no intention of becoming head No. 19. So he spoke to Poseidon about how to defeat Oenomaus. 'Seek the aid of Myrtilus the charioteer,' Poseidon said. 'He will help you tamper with the king's chariot. Just remember that he could take away the suitors' lives, but only you can take away their names from where they are displayed.'"

"Pelops found this confusing, but travelled to the court nonetheless. Oenomaus gave him a tour and made a big show of pointing out particular heads on the spires that he liked."

"Look there, on the eleventh tower – that one was Tricolonus! And on the fifteenth tower, the noble Aeolius! And see there on the ninth tower, it is Lasius! How handsome he still seems, despite the decay."

Finally Pelops was able to meet Myrtilus, and convinced him to help sabotage the king's chariot in exchange for half the kingdom and a night with Hippodamia. Once the sun set, and the palace slept, the two of them snuck to the stables where the chariots were kept.

However, Myrtilus had not anticipated that Oenomaus would have three potential chariots for the race the next day, each marked with a different number!

 Question: Which numbered chariot was the king going to use the next day?

a. 11-15-09   **b. 7-4-23**   **c. 1-8-3**

PERSEUS PART II:
FIFTY SHADES OF GRAEAE

Perseus offered to bring Polydectes any gift he desired.

"I want the head of the Gorgon Medusa," Polydectes replied.

Athena told Perseus he would have to seek the Graeae, three creatures that looked like old women: Pemphredo, Enyo and Persis.

They had only one eye and one tooth among the three of them. They agreed that at no point would any of them have both the eye and the tooth, and if they received one they would have to pass the other.

As Perseus approached, all three sat outside their lair looking to lure in victims. They were clustered around a pot in which some foul-smelling stew bubbled.

"I see a man approaches!" the first screeched.
"Who is it, Enyo?" asked the second.
"A stranger," said the first. "He looks tough."
"Hopefully not as tough as our last visitor,"
grunted the third Graia, chewing determinedly
on a piece of meat. "Let me see him."
"No, I want to see him!" said the second.
"My name is Perseus," he shouted as the three
women scrambled amongst themselves.
"Persis?" asked the second. "That's my name! You can't have it!"

46

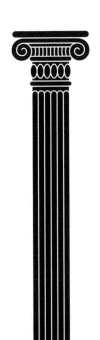

"Per-see-us," the first said. "And he can see
us. Though I can't see him now."
"Shut up and eat something," the third muttered,
then in a much sweeter voice she trilled, "Come, my
poor fellow, you must be tired after your journey."
"Ooh, he's handsome!" said the second.
"I will stand," said Perseus.
"You sound tired," the third continued. "Does he look tired?"
"See for yourself," the second said, touching
her face and throwing something.
"Be careful with that!" the third said. "Ah, yes. You must sit."
"Ptui!" spat the first. "Ooh, it came out.
Stick your hand in there and get it."
"Do it yourself!" said the second.
"Not you, her!" said the first.
"Maybe he can get it for us," said the
second. "Now that he's sat down."
"He hasn't," said the third.

Perseus realized he had to steal the eye if he was to force them to reveal the garden's location. So he sat carefully with the women, and waited for it to be passed.

The second woman said, "Just stick your hand in the pot there."

Perseus stuck his arm in the hot stew and got the tooth.

 Question: To which sister should he give the tooth: Pemphredo, Enyo or Persis?

PERSEUS PART III:
SNAKE GOOD HAIR OF YOURSELF

The Graeae finally revealed the location of Medusa. She dwelled within a ruined temple on Sarpedon, but despite her isolation she was still visited by many warriors hoping to vanquish her. She had been tragically transformed into her current form by Athena, and Perseus had heard tales that she was either incredibly beautiful or shockingly hideous, but he wondered if this ambiguity was yet another thing designed to drive people to look upon her.

He arrived at the temple and moved past the porch to the ranks of columns that formed the outside. These had fallen and were so tangled with vines and other plants that there was no way to enter but through the central doorway. Taking care not to look too closely, he observed that there were three main pathways through the broken stone and seats that led up to the furthest wall, where he could hear a laboured, rasping breath.

Now to put his plan into action. He took the mirrored shield of Athena that the Hesperides granted him and used it to see where Medusa was. The Gorgon sat on a throne against the furthest wall, apparently not seeing him, her face twisted in regret.

He also saw that the room was filled with what seemed at first to be statues but were clearly Medusa's previous victims – dozens of them!

Men, women, even some animals, all frozen in their poses of shock or dismay as they had looked upon her and turned to stone.

As long as he looked only at the mirror and not at her, Perseus could avoid their fate. But Medusa also clearly had incredible strength, speed and venomous snake hair, so Perseus also wanted to get to her without being seen.

Of the three pathways, the first had the most statues, an enormous cluster of them. The second had fewer statues, more widely spaced apart. And the third was almost empty, just a few here and there. A blind spot?

Gazing into the mirrored shield, he knew his presence here could not remain secret forever. Time to choose.

 Question: Which path should Perseus choose: the first, second or third?

PERSEUS PART IV:
GOING, GOING, GORGON

Perseus surged forward, and before Medusa could even move he decapitated her with his magical sword! The body plunged forward and as her venomous blood flowed onto the stone floor something incredible happened: two identical winged horses sprung from the blood, just as the Hesperides suggested!

But before Perseus could say anything to them, Medusa's severed head emitted one last, horrifying screech that echoed through the temple.

Then Perseus heard another snarling voice shout, "Sister? What has happened?" followed by a second howling, "We are coming!"

Perseus had not realized that the other two Gorgons, Euryale and Stheno, also dwelled here. They could also turn people to stone and, unlike Medusa, were immortal. Quickly putting her head in his sack, he saw the entrance to an underground tunnel and quickly darted inside.

But he'd been too late.

He heard Euryale's horrifying howl of despair followed by Stheno saying, "He went into the catacombs! Quickly, sister!"

He saw only one recourse: He quickly put on the helm of darkness, a gift from Hades that would grant him invisibility! But what Hades neglected to mention was that the helmet had no eyeholes! Perseus was now invisible, but also blind. A helm of darkness indeed.

Nonetheless he continued forward, using his sense of touch and his exceptionally sharp hearing, with the Gorgons screeching their confusion at his disappearance. He felt along the damp walls of the tunnel.

"We must stop him before he gets to the lake!" Stheno screeched, before being shushed by her sister.

A possible method of escape? He had heard the Gorgons could not step onto still water.

Eventually he came to a kind of crossroads. He could tell he was at the nexus of five different tunnels, all of which were possible exits, but he still could see nothing and the Gorgons were right behind him.

The first tunnel had the sound of whooshing waves. The second had the sound of dripping, glutinous slime. The third sounded like some kind of roaring fire. The fourth had the sound of cawing birds. And the fifth had some kind of sinister subterranean rumbling.

 Question: Which tunnel leads to the lake, and therefore escape?

PERSEUS PART V:
GET A HORSE

As he emerged onto the shores of the lake, he heard the angry cries of the Gorgons in the tunnels behind him. Removing his helm, he saw that the lake was huge, and he saw no way that he could return to the king to give him his prize.

It was at this point that the two winged horses, born from Medusa's blood, emerged from among some nearby trees. They approached Perseus warily.

The Hesperides had told him that upon Medusa's death these two stallions with wings would be created. One of them, Pegasus, would prove a faithful companion and fly him anywhere he desired, adventuring at his side once he stroked his mane. The other was his brother, Chrysaor, who would be immediately hostile to him and any human, attacking him if he dared touch him.

He would have to choose carefully – but the horses seemed identical except for a few small details. They both had blinding white coats and manes. The first horse had light brown eyes; wide, dark wings with pointed feather tips like an ostrich; and strong, muscular legs. The second had darker, redder eyes; a black diamond shape on his forehead; and multi-layered wings, like an eagle.

 Question: Which horse is Pegasus?

PERSEUS PART VI:
PERSEUS VS CETUS

Perseus now flew across the sky on the back of Pegasus, making his way back to Polydectes to show him Medusa's head. But as he flew over the coast of Aethiopia, he witnessed a young woman chained to a large rock.

He landed nearby and set about freeing her.

"You must go! Mother said she was more beautiful than the Nereids, the sea nymphs. And Poseidon was not happy. So he flooded the coast and sent a huge sea beast! Then mother consulted the oracle..."
"And the oracle told her to sacrifice you?" Perseus asked, still struggling with the chains.
"Yes."
"Seems like the oracle's main solution to everything," Perseus said, finally removing the chains.

The young woman introduced herself as Andromeda, but just as she stepped off the rock the enormous sea beast emerged from the water, howling and blowing water out of its blowhole. Cetus was a gargantuan whale with the head of a giant, enraged, snarling boar!

It immediately lunged for the two of them with its gaping mouth.

Perseus noted that its entire face was covered in sea creatures, with hundreds of barnacles on its tusks and its cavernous nostrils seemingly clogged with coral.

Perseus had to think fast, as the creature could swallow both of them without even needing to chew. He grabbed the chains that had bound Andromeda and, leaping into the air, whirled them around the beast's enormous jaws, binding them tightly shut!

The beast tumbled into the water, unable to release the chains. For minutes there was no sign except for a few bubbles, and he was ready to tell Andromeda to run before the beast suddenly reared up again, smashing into the shoreline and impeding their escape.

"I thought it would suffocate," said Perseus with confusion.
"I think you need this," said Andromeda, and with surprising strength she uprooted a small nearby tree.

 Question: What should Perseus do with the tree to defeat Cetus?

PERSEUS PART VII:
THE FINAL CHAPTER

As Perseus and Andromeda flew away on Pegasus they fell deeply in love, and they were resolved nothing would stand in their way.

Not Phineas, to whom Andromeda had already been promised in marriage by her parents, King Cepheus and Queen Cassiopeia. At Perseus and Andromeda's wedding, Phineas attacked Perseus, but Perseus defeated him without even touching him.

Not King Polydectes, who sent Perseus on the quest in the first place. He had heard of Perseus' success so, to try and hide from the hero, he had extinguished all the lights in his palace and covered all windows and doors so not a single beam of light could enter. But Perseus killed him and made his brother Dictys, the true love of his mother, the new king.

Not King Proetus, brother of Perseus' grandfather King Acrisius. He had forced Acrisius into exile and stolen his throne; and despite this, in broad daylight, Perseus killed him in seconds and restored the throne to Acrisius.

And not King Acrisius, who, seconds after thanking Perseus for restoring him to power, suffered the same fate as his brother. This was Perseus' final revenge for his grandfather exiling him and his mother, and the fulfilment of the prophecy that led to that exile in the first place.

What was the way that Perseus did this? The severed head of Medusa retained its ability to turn any who gazed at it to stone. But the truth is, one of the above people was not killed in this way.

 Question: Who did Perseus *not* turn to stone with Medusa's head?

Narcissus

Narcissus was a famous hunter, but it wasn't his ability to fire arrows or track prey that gave him fame; it was his incredible beauty.

His mother, Liriope, knew from his birth that his appearance was remarkable, and out of curiosity visited the seer Tiresias to ask about his future.

The old man said that Narcissus would live for a long time, "Only if he does not discover himself."

Liriope did not understand this at the time. So when, many years later, Narcissus was a fiercely handsome young man, she didn't worry about his incredible vanity.

"I am the most gorgeous in all creation," he would say in the mornings.

All the girls and many of the boys desired him, and every fashion choice he made became a trend. He parted his hair to the left and so did every man in the village. He wore a silver hair clasp on the right of his scalp and these items suddenly became a form of currency!

He took to wearing a single leather bracer on his left arm so he could rest his arrow on it when using his bow, and they had to kill the entire herd of cattle to keep up with the demand for these items.

But he rebuffed every single advance, saying he would know his true love when he saw them.

And so he did when one day he stopped to take a drink from a mountain pool and saw, swimming in it, the most beautiful youth he had ever seen.

He tried to tell the youth that they were the love of his life, even if they were wearing their bracer on the wrong arm, but they simply mouthed his own words back to him.

They could never be together because, as you may have already guessed, it was his own reflection. He wasted away staring at it and died by the pool, the ground spouting the gold and white flower that bears his name.

Why didn't he recognize his own reflection? Well, he was remarkably stupid. But there is another reason.

 Question: Why didn't Narcissus think the youth in the pool was him?

HYPNOS

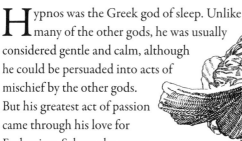

Hypnos was the Greek god of sleep. Unlike many of the other gods, he was usually considered gentle and calm, although he could be persuaded into acts of mischief by the other gods. But his greatest act of passion came through his love for Endymion. Selene, the moon goddess, adored him too, but Hypnos sought the young man for himself. In some retellings, Hypnos let Endymion sleep with his eyes open, so he could gaze upon him during this time. But other myths say that Hypnos' love caused Endymion to sleep more and more until eventually he never woke again.

If we imagine we are using the 24-hour clock, on the first day Endymion was awake for 6 out of every 8 hours.

On the second day, he slept double the time he slept the day before.

On the third day, he slept 3 times the amount he slept the first day.

On the fourth day, he slept the total of the hours he was awake the first day, plus the total of the hours he was awake the third.

On the fifth day, he slept twice the amount he slept on the second day.

And on the sixth day, he slept 4 times the amount he slept on the first.

 Question: From which day was he no longer awake at any time?

SISYPHUS

Sisyphus was the first king of Ephyra and was notorious for repeatedly defying the gods, whether it was by killing his guests (and therefore breaking the Greek tradition of *xenia,* or hospitality) or by tricking the various gods and denizens of the Underworld into releasing him. After managing to anger Zeus, Ares, Hermes and Hades, Sisyphus was sentenced to his famous punishment: to roll a boulder up an enormous hill in the Underworld. As soon as he got close to the top the boulder was enchanted to roll back down to the bottom again, making his punishment theoretically eternal, and inventing the adjective "Sisyphean" for a task that is futile or unending.

As decades, then centuries, passed, the endless drama of the gods and the chthonic residents meant that Sisyphus was almost forgotten. When clearing out his realm to accommodate the new casualties of an immense war, Hades was extinguishing several streams of magma when he suddenly came across Sisyphus sitting next to his boulder at the bottom of the hill.

Sisyphus' brow was sweaty and his hands bore many scars. His clothes were stained and torn from centuries of toil, but still intact. His boulder, five times his size and pitted with cracks, moss and blood stains from his hands, was at rest next to him. He eyed Hades with a look both cunning and maddened by isolation.

"Why are you not pushing the boulder, penitent?"
Hades intoned in his rumbling voice.
"It has just rolled back down the hill," Sisyphus panted.
"And I was resting for a few moments before beginning the next push."
"No," said Hades grimly. "You have not pushed it for years. Perhaps decades."

 Question: How does Hades know that Sisyphus has not been pushing the boulder up the hill?

The Adventures of Bellerophon Part I: Xenia and the Warrior Prince

Bellerophon's origins are murkier than those of other mythical heroes, but it is widely agreed that he was the child of Queen Eurynome, and his father may have been Poseidon. He was exiled from his home kingdom for the murder of Belleros, but any detail of who that might be has been lost to history.

In his exile, Bellerophon went to visit King Proetus, who was able to cleanse him of his disgrace. But he soon ended up in disgrace again when Proetus' wife falsely accused him of attacking her.

The ancient Greeks followed a principle known as *xenia,* or "guest-friendship" – a ritualized form of hospitality born out of Zeus' status as the god of guests, and also being rather fond of throwing lightning around. It was also a good idea as the gods would often walk in disguise among mortals.

Under xenia, hosts had to provide food, drink, accommodation and other amenities as well as give gifts, and not ask a person's name or business until these had been provided, because it had to be unconditional.

They also couldn't kill their guests, like Prometheus did. The guest, in turn, had to accept any offered hospitality, tell stories of their lives and the world, and not overstay their welcome!

Proetus wanted to kill Bellerophon, but as he was his guest he could not. But he thought he'd found a loophole. He wrote a tablet to his father-in-law, King Iobates, detailing Bellerophon's supposed crime and asking Iobates to remove him from the world. He sealed it and gave it to Bellerophon, asking him to deliver it to Iobates, reasoning that, as he was not his guest, Iobates could kill Bellerophon for him!

However, when Iobates read the message he found himself unable to kill Bellerophon too.

Question: Why couldn't King Iobates kill Bellerophon?

THE ADVENTURES OF BELLEROPHON PART II: CAPTURING PEGASUS

Finding himself in the same bind that Proetus was in, King Iobates fell back on what had become an increasingly popular way to try and sidestep *xenia:* Challenging your guest to defeat a monster!

Iobates asked Bellerophon to defeat the Chimera, a vicious monster terrorizing the countryside of the nearby region of Caria. Obligated to comply, and eager to impress Iobates' daughter Philonoe, Bellerophon set out, and on the way met the seer Polyeidos of Corinth. The seer advised that if Bellerophon wanted any chance to defeat the creature, he should try to capture the famous Pegasus, who had taken to living wild in the area after its adventures with Perseus.

The flying horse could not be captured in the air, so Bellerophon would have to wait until it landed. Pegasus' eyrie was inaccessible, so it would have to be when the beast stopped to drink. Even when it did so, though, Bellerophon knew Pegasus was wild and strong and liable to attack him if on peak form. Athena gave him a golden bridle, which would calm the beast – but he had to get it on Pegasus first.

Bellerophon knew that Pegasus had three preferred watering places. The first was in a shady glen surrounded by trees, their branches groaning with fruit; but none dared pick it, so it rotted and fermented on the branches, only occasionally falling into the otherwise clean water.

The second was a rushing river near a wide plain, with only sparse foliage dotting the landscape.

The third was a waterfall in an area thick with other wild animals, which would also come to the drinking hole. They tolerated Pegasus' presence, but would react to Bellerophon with aggression or fear.

 Question: Which place would be best for Bellerophon to capture Pegasus?

The Adventures of Bellerophon Part III: The Chimera

Once he was wearing the bridle, Pegasus was considerably calmed, and seemed happy to be accompanying a hero on their adventures once again. Now to find the lair of the Chimera...

The beast was an unnatural union of three different animals. It had a lion's head and body; a goat's head that could breathe fire sprouted from its back; and instead of a tail it had a huge, venomous snake with incredibly sharp teeth.

The term "chimera" has latterly been used to describe any such hybrid animal in folklore or legend, and there are many in Greek and Roman mythology, although most are a mix of only two animals. There were Satyrs that were half human, half goat (humans are animals, of course), and Centaurs that were half human, half horse. Pegasus was a mix of horse and bird, and the Echidna (whose name was later given to a real animal) was half human, half snake. And of course we have the half-lion, half-bird Griffin, and the vicious half-human, half-bird Harpies.

 Question: If we imagine these creatures randomly lettered A to F, can you work out which is which, using the following clues?

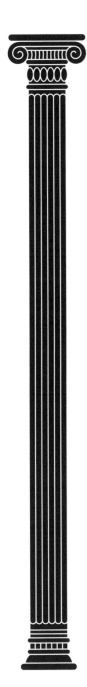
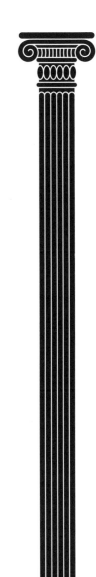

- Creature B has no animal in common with the Chimera.
- Creature A shares one animal with the Chimera and one with Creature B.
- A, B, C and D all have the same animal.
- Creature E shares one common animal with Creature F, but has no common animal with Creature A.
- Creature C has hooves.

The Adventures of Bellerophon Part IV: Eat Lead, Chimera!

Bellerophon stopped at a small camp and learned from the men there that the Chimera was nearby. Setting off, he approached the lair from the air while riding Pegasus and shouted for the creature to emerge. After a second, the Chimera came leaping out of the cave, all three heads snarling! Bellerophon flew just out of the range of its attack, dodging the blasts of fiery breath from its goat head. But, while it couldn't hurt him, Bellerophon found that he couldn't hurt it either! Any arrows he fired were immolated in moments. Any weapons he threw were dodged expertly or simply bitten into pieces by its powerful jaws.

Ultimately, he realized how to defeat the creature. If he put a large piece of lead on the end of his spear, the beast's fiery breath would melt the metal as it was inside its mouth, choking it. But where could he get lead so quickly? Its soft nature meant that – while Greeks sometimes used it in its pure form for lamps and small statues, and on tablets as a writing medium – it was usually alloyed with bronze to make it stronger.

Back in the camp, he found that most of the metallic objects there were alloys, and unsuitable. He had to act fast before the beast came and killed any of the men. Then a messenger arrived with a letter from Iobates suggesting that if Bellerophon took any longer, he would assume he had run away in cowardice! Looking at this message, Bellerophon knew he had found his answer.

 Question: What did Bellerophon use to defeat the Chimera?

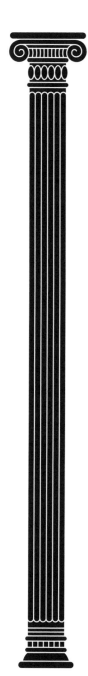

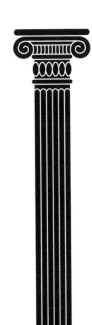

PART V:
BOLDER ADVENTURES

The monster defeated, Bellerophon rode Pegasus back to the court of King Iobates with its head as evidence. Iobates, not to be thwarted, decided to instead send Bellerophon on more and more dangerous errands, fighting pirates and armies and, in one infamous episode, the Amazons.

Bellerophon's triumphs were much more the result of his cunning than his martial ability, and defeating the Amazons was going to be difficult. He had been unable to face them one on one, or even engage them at all without being spotted! But he had Pegasus, and therefore an unfair advantage.

Loading Pegasus up with a small variety of boulders in a net, he used the beast's incredible strength and superb flying ability to dive-bomb the surprised warrior women. He aimed to get them to surrender in confusion as quickly as possible before they realized what was happening or how to counter it. But he had been uncertain whether to use heavier boulders to injure and kill as many Amazons as possible, or lighter ones to allow him to drop more of them in a short period of time.

In the end he decided to use both, levelling a 1kg boulder at the queen and a 5kg boulder at her second in command.

 Question: If neither woman moves, and both boulders are dropped at exactly the same time from exactly the same height, which Amazon would be hit first?

PART VI:
THE STING

After Bellerophon defeated the Amazons, Iobates decided he could no longer try to defeat him and, upon learning of Proetus' wife's deception, permitted Bellerophon to marry his daughter.

For a while, all was well. Bellerophon and Philonoe had many children, and Bellerophon settled down to help rule the kingdom.

But his memories of his victories caused him to become arrogant. He had tamed Pegasus! Killed the Chimera! Defeated the Amazons! His father was a god. Surely he, too, should dwell on Olympus.

So one day he saddled up Pegasus and set out across the sky to fly up to Olympus and claim his place in the pantheon!

The Olympian gods, however, disagreed. A hero may do many great deeds, but it does not make them a god. They discussed attacking him with wind, lightning or many terrible monsters. But

in the end Zeus decided the best message was to send a tiny insect to fly and sting Pegasus. When this happened, Bellerophon was thrown immediately and fell many miles to the ground. Whether he died or lived in agony is widely disputed. Pegasus himself arrived at Olympus and was immediately claimed by Zeus to carry his thunderbolts while he was roaming.

But which tiny creature did Zeus send? When he put out a call among the mini beasts of Olympus, five answered: a spider, a housefly, an ant, a butterfly and a hoverfly.

 Question: Which insect did Zeus choose to sting Pegasus?

DEMETER AND PERSEPHONE

Demeter was the goddess of agriculture, in particular grains like wheat and other seasonal crops. The Eleusinian Mysteries that Hercules studied to gain access to the Underworld told of her daughter Persephone's abduction by Hades. He was infatuated with her, and Zeus gave him permission to take her. But Demeter was so enraged and upset by this that she made it so nothing could grow anywhere across the world, and set off searching for her daughter.

The god's worshippers starving in the bleak, famine-ridden landscape meant that Zeus had to order Hades to return Persephone. But Hades tricked Persephone into eating something and, by the laws of the Underworld, if you eat any food there you are obliged to remain. However, as the food was only six pomegranate seeds, Persephone was required to remain there for just six months.

So every year Persephone would spend six months on the surface world with her mother, then travel back to the Underworld, and Demeter's despair would cause the land to become cold and plants to stop growing, die or hibernate. This is what caused the seasons of autumn and winter.

Of course, Demeter's despair did not mean that nothing at all grew. In fact, some plants, like evergreen trees, were blessed by her and had magical properties. There are even some plants, including brassicas, that would seem to defy the forces of time. There is a tale of a type of chard that was sown in 1798, and yet grew and was reaped in 1797.

 Question: How is it possible for seeds planted in 1798 to result in plants in 1797?

PIECES OF PELOPS

One of the reasons why Greek heroes – even those who were children of the gods – were not welcomed in Olympus was the actions of one of Zeus' children, King Tantalus.

He was brought to the table at Olympus and given food and drink by the gods. But Tantalus considered himself cleverer than the gods, and stole ambrosia and nectar to give to his people.

While this could be seen as an act of charity, or a rebalancing of power, Tantalus' main crime was much worse. He wanted to learn if the gods were truly as omniscient as they claimed. But rather than engage them in a game of "guess which hand the coin is in," he chose to murder his son Pelops, chop him up and serve him to the gods as a stew.

This horrific act was to no avail, as the gods did in fact realize what he had done and refused to eat the stew (except for Demeter, who was distracted by the situation with Persephone and accidentally ate Pelops' shoulder). Tantalus was immediately thrown into the Underworld for a particularly grim punishment, and the parts of Pelops were given to Clotho, one of the Moirai, or Fates. They were the personification of people's destiny and, as such, had incredible powers, and the gods knew that this was not the final fate of poor Pelops.

Clotho got her magic cauldron and put the pieces inside, boiling them again in a magical fluid that would reconnect them. But she had to get them in the right order, which was:

1: Head; 2: Neck; 3: Torso; 4: Arms; 5: Hands; 6: Legs; 7: Feet

But as she put them in, she saw that they were in this order:

5: Hands; 3: Torso; 4: Arms; 1: Head; 7: Feet; 2: Neck; 6: Legs

However, Clotho knew that every time she stirred the magic cauldron, any body part that was a lower number than the one to its left would move left by one. Each body part would only move once per stir, unless of course displaced by another one moving left.

 Question: How many times would Clotho have to stir the cauldron before Pelops' body was in the right order?

The Torment of Tantalus

Tantalus' punishment in the Underworld was uniquely harsh, so much so that the word "tantalizing" has its origins in this myth.

He was cursed to stand with his feet in a pool of clear, fresh water underneath the branches of an enormous, lush tree on which grew the juiciest fruit imaginable. But if he ever tried to reach up with his hands to grab the fruit, the branches of the tree would lift up out of his reach, no matter how high he jumped. The fruit would never fall off naturally, either, or be shaken off by anything.

Furthermore, if he tried to bend down to drink the cool water, it would drain away from him, even if he literally laid down on the bottom of the pool. For centuries he had to remain like this, unable to leave, as a giant rock hung over him and would crush him if he ever left the pool, and he would immediately return, still starving and emaciated but unable to die.

What Tantalus didn't realize, however, was that there was a way he could have had some of the fruit – a loophole in the curse that he never discovered.

 Question: How could Tantalus have had some of the fruit?

a. Shake the tree.

b. Climb the tree.

c. Stand on his head.

d. Crouch down and leap up quickly.

e. Jump out of the pool so that the boulder hits the tree.

A ZEUS CONNECTION

One of the interesting consequences of the gods having so many children but being functionally immortal (or at least incredibly long-lived) is that their children spanned many generations. Centuries could pass between some of the Greek heroes who were sired by different gods at different times.

In some situations, these heroes were even said to be descended from each other, both as a sign of their own "pedigree" and as a recognition of the interconnectedness of their mythological world and their journey.

One of the biggest ones was that Hercules was said to be descended from Perseus. Some accounts say that he was his great-grandson. But as they were both the sons of Zeus, that means they were also half-brothers.

This puts Zeus in an interesting but probably not unique situation of being related to himself.

 Question: Based on this information, what relation is Zeus to himself in this scenario?

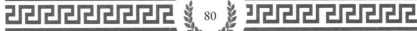

Jason and the Argonauts
The Argonauts Part I: The Crew

Another famous mythological saga is that of Jason and his crew's journey in the *Argo* to get the Golden Fleece.

Jason's birth was originally kept secret, as his uncle Pelias had usurped his father Aeson's throne and killed all his descendants. Sent away for his protection by his mother, he returned to confront his uncle when he was a man. On the way, he lost a sandal in a river, and as Pelias had heard from an oracle that a one-sandalled man would kill him and inherit his kingdom, he knew who Jason was. But once again, according to the rules of hospitality, Pelias could not have him executed. So instead he set Jason a challenge: If he brought him the Golden Fleece, he could have the kingdom.

Jason quickly arranged for a boat to be built: the *Argo,* named after its designer, Argus. And he knew he'd need a large crew, as he was not beloved by the gods (or so he thought) and would need their help at every turn.

His crew was about 50 men, but if you read the following five descriptions, you will realize that one of them could not have been on board:

1. *Orpheus: Legendary bard and court musician, who later descended into the Underworld to retrieve his love, Eurydice.*
2. *Hercules: The famous warrior, he of the 12 labours.*
3. *Autolycus: Compatriot of Hercules and later the founder of Sinope.*
4. *Perseus: The hero, defeater of Medusa and rider of Pegasus.*
5. *Castor and Pollux: The famous twins, known in Latin as the constellation Gemini.*

 Question: Which of these men was not an Argonaut?

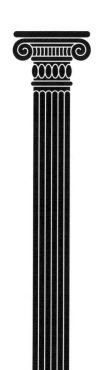

THE ARGONAUTS PART II: ARGO ROW

The *Argo* had many amenities, including different types of sacred wood and a legendary prow that could speak with a human voice and tell oracles.

Some storytellers claim it was the first boat; this has been contradicted by multiple other sources, but it can be agreed that it was an advanced ship with special sails. However, it could not rely on these to convey it all the way, as the crew's protection came primarily from Hera; and Poseidon, while not planning to sink the vessel, also had no particular interest in its success, as Pelias was his son. For that reason, the Argonauts found themselves becalmed and had to resort to the boat's second form of propulsion: two rows of 25 oars each side, to be rowed by the 50 men.

At first they made good progress. But as water supplies dwindled and the sun beat down, the men found themselves delirious and close to passing out. Twenty-five of them collapsed and were unable to row, and the 25 who remained, after attending to their comrades, sat down and did their best to try to row to dry land, which was 100km away.

But strangely, when there were 50 men feeling strong, they progressed about 30km toward dry land in two hours. When the same 50 were feeling weaker, they managed to travel about 15km toward dry land in the same time. But when the 25 men sat down they found that, despite rowing at about the same speed, they could not make any progress at all toward dry land.

 Question: Assuming that Poseidon had not played a trick on them or blown wind against them, why could the 25 Argonaut rowers not make any progress?

THE ARGONAUTS PART III: CYZICUS' PARTY

After a brief, somewhat shameful detour to the island of Lemnos, the Argonauts found themselves among the Doliones, a coastal tribe whose king, Cyzicus, extended incredible hospitality to them. He was in fact delighted to meet so many great warriors, in particular some of the famous heroes whom the Argonauts counted amongst their number. Orpheus even composed a new song in honour of the tribe and their remarkable generosity.

The Argonauts intended to go past Bear Mountain, and the king fully intended to tell them what lived in the land beyond there. It was occupied by the Gegeines, a cluster of six-armed giants who hated humans – except as a mid-morning snack. But the king was distracted at the huge party he threw for the group and neglected to mention this fact. And because of this, while Jason led the majority of the group into the forest to look for more supplies, their ship was ambushed, and it was only with Hercules' intervention that the giants could be defeated.

As they hung their palace with black cloth and doused their lights in premature mourning of the horrible fate the Argonauts would suffer, the king was asked why he had neglected to tell them about the murderous giants. Cyzicus could only splutter that he had been enraptured in conversation with one of the Argonauts:

"He has done so much… He's been a drover and a musician, a weightlifter and a spelunker – even a hydrological engineer!"

 Question: Which Argonaut is he talking about: Orpheus, Jason or Hercules?

THE ARGONAUTS PART IV: JOURNEY INTO DARKNESS

A fter their terrifying encounter with the giants, the Argonauts were rattled, but also slightly resentful of the Doliones. How could they not have warned them about the Gegeines? But Jason reminded them that the Doliones may have been unaware of the giants.

"They live to the south of the mountains and may never have ventured past them to this land. The Argo *allowed us to come to their lands, but they have no vessel of their own. They are not explorers or adventurers."*

Finding no way forward, the Argonauts decided to board the now somewhat damaged *Argo* and sail from the beach they were on, west of the Gegeines' camp. It was incredibly dark, without even the stars to guide them, but they feared remaining and facing other unknown threats.

They kept sailing west but then decided to tack south, then further west, before coming back east almost as far as they had gone west and finally heading to the north, where they found another beach. As they disembarked they found the land to be just as dark as the sea, and when a cry went up from a guard, the now paranoid Argonauts launched into battle and were joined in their energy by the armed forces of the place where they had just landed.

It was only once the fight was over and their opponents lay dead on the ground that the Argonauts realized what a terrible thing had happened.

 Question: Why was it terrible that the Argonauts had killed their mysterious opponents?

THE ARGONAUTS PART V: POLLUX VS AMYCUS

The Argonauts continued on their series of unfortunate events, having strange encounters and mysterious adventures. They came to the land of the Bebryces, who were ruled over by the arrogant, seemingly indestructible King Amycus.

Amycus, a son of Poseidon, was rude and aggressive and widely disliked. His worst quality was that anyone who came within his kingdom who he took personal offence to – which was most – he would challenge to a boxing match.

> *"Look at these pathetic worms!" he roared as the Argonauts*
> *entered the king's combination throne room/boxing ring.*
> *"Where is Hercules, the so-called mighty hero?"*
> *"He left us a few adventures back," said Jason, eyeing Amycus warily.*
> *"So the coward didn't have the guts to face me? He's been*
> *to the Underworld but couldn't square up to little old me?*
> *I wanted to share reminiscences of seeing Charon..."*
> *"I'm pretty sure he's never heard of you," said Pollux dismissively.*
> *Amycus glared at Pollux with gritted teeth.*
> *"YOU. In the ring, now."*

Pollux squared up against the king. Even though he was twice Pollux's age, Amycus looked in incredible health. And as they began trading blows, nothing Pollux did could seem to hurt Amycus. Every blow landed seemed to have no effect, while Amycus' punches were seriously damaging Pollux.

"You could hit me with the whole Argo *and it wouldn't even bruise my little finger, boy!" Amycus* gloated. *"Ever since my mother took me by the arm and washed me, I can beat any man in the ring!"*

Pollux was weakening, his left arm broken; but then he remembered something the oracular mast of the *Argo* had whispered to him once. It was the tale of a young warrior who would be born generations from now, who would gain great strength from an unexpected source – but with it, an unusual weakness.

Pollux wound up his right arm and in a swift blow hit Amycus precisely on... the elbow! And yet somehow this one punch immediately killed the king! He dropped to the floor of the ring like a sack of olives.

Question: How did Pollux know that hitting Amycus' elbow would kill him?

THE ARGONAUTS PART VI: PHINEAS AND HERBS

Finally the Argonauts came to a temple in Salmydessus where the seer, Phineas, lived. He had been cursed with blindness by Zeus for daring to use his powers to reveal the activities of the gods. And for continuing to use his powers in defiance of this, he had been beset with the "hounds of Zeus" known as the Harpies, half-human, half-bird monsters that constantly hovered over where he lived.

The people of the town still cared for Phineas, and although they could not come near his temple for fear of being attacked by the monsters, they would come daily and leave food and water for him on a table at the edge of the entrance.

However, as soon as Phineas touched the food, the Harpies would descend! They could not attack him personally, but they would eat as much as they could and befoul anything left!

"Why do they not attack you?" Jason asked Phineas once they came to the temple and found him sitting on the steps, looking barely more than skin and bones. "Apollo, he who gave me the gift of prophecy, could not restore my sight nor drive away the Harpies, but he has given me this chiton that the Harpies find repulsive to their touch and taste, so they cannot attack me directly. But they hound me nonetheless, attacking all around me and taking any food I try to eat. And the chiton is falling apart as well."

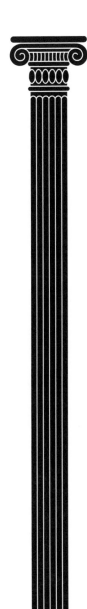

Phineas scratched his arm and little threads
and pieces of the chiton flaked off.
Jason nodded. "Worry not, old man. We shall find a way to
kill these creatures. But how long have they hounded you?"
"Nigh on 10 years now," he sighed.
"And yet you are still alive, even though they always
attack the instant you approach the food?"
Phineas tapped his nose. "Well... let me just say I have a special
herb that makes one or two of the foods inedible to the Harpies."

 **Question: What is Phineas' secret ingredient to keep
the Harpies away from some of the food?**

THE ARGONAUTS PART VII: THE DOVE FROM ABOVE

Luckily two of the Argonauts, Zetes and Calais, had winged feet and helmets, and so were able to pursue the Harpies through the air and slay them with ease. Thus released from his curse, Phineas happily explained the precise route the Argonauts must take to get to the Golden Fleece.

This route would, however, be perilous, and the most dangerous part would be from the clashing rocks. These two cliffs lay at the end of a narrow inlet and – through means magical or physical – would clash together at a regular pace, crushing anything that tried to pass between them! It was very difficult for the Argonauts to judge whether, even with the magical assistance and heroic efforts of its crew, they could make it through the rocks without being crushed.

"It is not easy to see through the myths, but I can say that at rest they stand about 500km apart," said Autolycus, using modern measurements to help avoid confusion.

"Every five minutes they begin rushing together, and it takes only two minutes for them to smash into each other. They stay that way for a mere five seconds and then pull apart at the same speed, returning to their previous space."
"How long is the face of each cliff?" Jason asked.
"From here I cannot tell," Autolycus said sadly. "The Argo *is 30m long."*

A plan was formed to see if the cliffs were survivable. One of the Argonauts had a pet dove, an adult male 30cm long (10cm of that being its tail), and it was decided that they would sail as close to the edge of where the cliffs met as they could and release the dove, seeing if it would survive the passage through the cliffs. At the moment just after the cliffs had clashed and were coming apart, Jason released the bird and it flew directly forward as fast as it could, and as the cliffs hurtled toward each other the entire crew gasped as the dove was suddenly blocked from view by their collision.

Minutes later, the dove returned to the boat alive. However, it was now missing its tail, which they realized had been caught between the clashing rocks at the last second!

 Question: If the dove flew at its top speed of 60km/h through the cliffs, and the *Argo* normally travelled at about 30km/h (much faster than most boats of its type), at about what minimum speed would the *Argo* need to travel to survive the clashing rocks?

THE ARGONAUTS PART VIII: DEATH IN THE WILD

The Argonauts rested briefly in the court of King Lycus, who supported them greatly as they had killed King Amycus. Amycus had been a fool to Lycus on multiple occasions, including pretending to hold his hand out to shake it, and then pulling it back at the last minute and adjusting his hair instead.

While there, a few of the Argonauts ventured into a nearby forest for hunting and upon return had dire news: Idmon had been slain.

This was not necessarily surprising to the group, because Idmon had prophetic abilities, and he had foreseen his own death on the journey yet had still joined up out of a sense of adventure and destiny.

"How did he die?" asked Jason. "I remember he said he saw he would be slain by a mighty warrior who bore two curved spears! They were short and very hirsute, with a mighty, matted beard! They would stab him in the thighs, and then relentlessly keep attacking until he fell! The warrior was from the same tribe that once contended with Hercules, and a half-brother of theirs also fought Perseus near the coast..."
"Well," said one of the other hunters, "that does describe his killer. In a way."

 Question: Who, or what, killed Idmon?

90

THE ARGONAUTS PART IX: STYMPHALIAN RESURRECTION

Once again aboard the *Argo,* the crew felt relief that their journey must almost be at an end; what else could possibly beset them?

The answer, they soon found, was the Stymphalian birds that Hercules once faced! After that mighty warrior had scared them with the incredible sound of the *krotala* rattle, they'd fled the swamp they'd been living in and found a new habitat on the island of Aretias, attacking passing boats by firing their razor-sharp feathers at them like arrows, then feasting on any murdered sailors.

Unfortunately, Hercules was no longer with the Argonauts, and even if he had been, he had told them he no longer had the rattle, having dropped it somewhere in the Underworld, "probably in the Styx or something."

Luckily, the Argonauts still had some shields to protect themselves from the feathers – but not enough to protect everyone. And their arrows bounced off uselessly, as did their spears.

They had to resort to hunkering down on the deck behind their shields as the birds' relentless onslaught of feathers made a rat-a-tat noise on the shields, like hail on a tin roof.

"Maybe if one came closer we could stab it between the feathers, like so!" said Castor, jabbing Jason's shield with his spear and making a loud clanging noise.
"They won't descend," Jason replied. "But I might have a… musical idea."

 Question: How can the Argonauts scare away the Stymphalian birds?

91

THE ARGONAUTS PART X:
YOKE THE BULLS

The Argonauts finally arrived at the location of the Golden Fleece! Now they had to convince King Aeetes to relinquish it. The king had been told by an oracle that if he gave up the fleece he would lose his kingdom, so it was guarded by an enormous dragon with 100 razor-sharp teeth.

Luckily the *xenia* hospitality tradition meant that Aeetes could not directly deny the fleece to the Argonauts.

"That old thing? Of course you can have it!" he said. "I just need you to do me a little kindness. I need you to yoke my bulls. They were given to me by Hephaestus, and they are enormous, with brazen feet and nostrils that shoot fire. And they attack most things on sight. Animals, people, anything they've set on fire... but not ordinary objects, it seems."

Jason tried multiple times to sneak up on the bulls, from behind curtains and at night-time with no lights. But they always saw him immediately and came roaring at him, and it was the same for every other Argonaut. The only time they paused was once when Pollux leapt out at them from a cool lake they were drinking at; but after brief confusion, they once again attacked.

Luckily Jason had an advantage of sorts: Hera was well disposed to Jason and asked Aphrodite to send dreams about him to Medea, a high priestess who also happened to be the daughter of the king.

"I have watched carefully, and I know how to protect you from the
bulls, so you can get closer and yoke them without them attacking you."
said Hera. "It's this thick wool blanket – put it over your head."
"Will it make me invisible?" asked Jason.
"In a way. But not with magic."
"I'm feeling very hot in here!" he said in a muffled voice.
"As long as that's where it stays, then you'll be fine," she said knowingly.

 Question: Why will the blanket enable Jason to be invisible to the bulls?

THE ARGONAUTS PART XI: SHOULDN'T SOWING DRAGON'S TEETH GIVE YOU DRAGONS?

King Aeetes seemed suspiciously pleased when Jason presented him with his newly yoked brazen-footed bulls. He ordered them personally attached to his royal plough, and then rode them up and down the fields outside, ploughing up the dirt and throwing some kind of large white objects into the ground.

"I have one more challenge for you, Argonauts," Aeetes said, grinning, and they watched in horror as 100 armed, grey-skinned human warriors grew up out of the field like corn. They marched implacably into the courtyard and stood silently awaiting the king's orders, with looks of hatred on their faces. "Grown from dragon's teeth! They are skilled and ferocious and looking for any reason to attack. I'm not a complete monster, so I'll give you two minutes to hide, and then my warriors will hunt you, and you must see to it that they all die. Then the fleece will be yours!"

Seeing no alternative, Jason and his men immediately ran in several directions, taking up positions in different parts of the palace. Medea sought out Jason again.

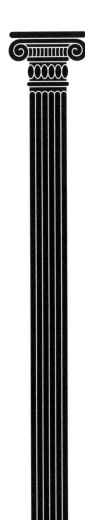

"These warriors may seem inhuman, but their passion
and rage are real," she said. "And I have noticed that,
although they seem identical, there are in fact two factions;
they have split almost into two groups. Maybe it was
the top teeth and the bottom teeth? I don't know."

"How does that aid us?" Jason asked desperately.

"If you can make the two groups fight each other, they will
mostly wipe themselves out before they even raise a sword to you!
Don't you have any experience of allies killing each other?"

"So how do I do it?" asked Jason quickly, avoiding the subject.

"It's best to strike now, before they leave the central
courtyard. See the two groups? All you need do is throw
a stone to strike one of the warriors and they will assume
it came from the other group. Then it will escalate."

But Jason needed to know which way to throw the rock.

"If I throw it to the left, I can strike the leader of the first group
square on. If I throw it into the middle, I could miss entirely
– but there's a chance it will ricochet off the central pillar and
hit one of the soldiers in the second group. And if I throw it
to the right, I can't hit the second group's leader, but I can
probably strike and even kill the soldier right next to him."

 **Question: In which direction should Jason throw
the rock?**

THE ARGONAUTS PART XII: HOW TO TAME HIS DRAGON

K ing Aeetes looked around at 100 dragon-tooth warriors, his countenance grave.

"Where are the Argonauts?" he muttered to his son, Apsyrtus.
"Medea has taken them to the shrine, father," Apsyrtus said
with clenched teeth. "Shall we dispatch more forces?"
"Go to the Argo *and make a pyre of it. But do not go to the*
shrine. My dragon will make swift work of them."
It was true that Aeetes' dragon had killed many; the shrine was littered
with the bones of warriors. But the dragon was now asleep, having been
tricked into eating a sheep laced with a potion that Medea had concocted.
"It took the beast much longer to eat the sheep than I thought
it would," she said. "But you can now get the fleece."
As Jason stepped forward, Medea threw her hands out.
"WAIT! You cannot touch the dragon. If you do,
it might stir and attack you in its sleep."

*"But I don't see how I can get the fleece without touching it," Jason
said, pointing out how it blocked all four possible paths.*

Its tail blocked the first path and was covered in poisonous spikes that would
kill a man the instant they touched them. Its back legs blocked the second, and
they had razor-sharp claws that could decapitate you in moments. Its front legs
blocked the third, and the claws on them were somehow even longer and sharper!
Its immense head blocked the fourth – and although its mouth was closed in
almost a smile of slumber, Jason had heard many stories of warriors chewed up by
its 100 infamous sword-like teeth.

 Question: Which path would be the safest for Jason to use?

THE ARGONAUTS PART XIII: CIRCE'S BACK

As Medea and the Argonauts fled to the *Argo* bearing the magical Golden Fleece, they found Medea's brother Apsyrtus waiting for them. His men had not yet begun to burn the *Argo,* but they stood firm against the warriors.

Jason drew his sword, but Medea stopped his hand.

"Wait, Jason! You cannot strike a blow against
him; you are still my father's guest!"
Medea took Jason's sword as her brother stepped forward, smirking.
"But I can!" she suddenly exclaimed, and with superhuman
speed spun around and sliced her brother into five pieces!

Apsyrtus' men were so shocked that they were taken off guard by the Argonauts and quickly dispatched. They got onto the ship and were soon away, but found themselves in the middle of an enormous tsunami.

"Zeus is angry," intoned the ship's prophetic stern. "The
blow was struck with Jason's sword, and so he must
take the test of purity before you can proceed."

The only person who could purify them was Circe, the minor goddess, who lived on an island nearby. With great difficulty they made their way there and found her in her house, smiling with wicked amusement.

"You seek to purify yourself of this murder? Very well, I have no love for this Apsyrtus. But I have no love for thee too, Jason. So here is my test."

She placed in front of them three identical bottles with three identically purple liquids inside.

"One of these bottles has my sacred potion for purifying transgressions. The other two will change you into a pig or a goat. If you are fated to be purified, you will choose correctly!"

Jason peered at the bottles. There was no indication of any differences whatsoever. He shrugged and reached out to grab bottle 1, but then Circe held up her hand.

"Wait!"

Circe picked up bottle 2 and, with a flourish, flung its contents over Iphitos, one of the other Argonauts. With a strange bleating shriek his arms twisted into legs and his skin grew grey fur. After a few seconds, he was a strangely placid goat.

Circe replaced the empty bottle and fixed Jason with a stare, indicating bottles 1 and 3 with her hands.

"Now…do you wish to change your mind?"

Jason thought carefully.

 Question: Is there any advantage to be had from Jason changing his mind?

The Argonauts Part XIV: Sirens' Song

They returned to the *Argo* and set sail to return to King Pelias, who, you may recall, sent them on this quest to begin with. Their voyage would take them past the Sirens – the part-woman, part-bird creatures whose magically alluring voices would cause all who heard them to willingly go to their own death!

At the beginning, when they were assembling the crew for the *Argo*, Jason was told by the ship's prophetic mast that Orpheus, the famous musician, should join their crew. Jason knew not why, as he had been very ineffective at rowing, fighting and navigating. But as they heard the first strains of the Sirens' song in the distance and began to feel its call, Orpheus ordered them to turn about and stop for a while.

"I've heard enough of the Sirens' tune," Orpheus said. "I can write something that will counter it. My melody will cancel out their voices so totally, we could sail the Argo *right onto their laps and they couldn't do anything about it. But I have to get it down on a tablet first."*

As we have little evidence of the true ancient Greek musical scale, we will say that Orpheus used a numerical music system.

"I counter tunes by playing another one that's got a special connection to the original note," he said to a barely comprehending Jason. "So if they're belting out 4-10-6-3-8, I can play 2-5-3-1-4 and they're history!"

"Yes," said Jason, shaking his head.

Orpheus finished writing down the Sirens' melody; it was 5-11-7-2-13.

"Ah," he said. "Wow. What a bummer."

Question: Which five numbers should Orpheus play to counter the Sirens' tune?

THE ARGONAUTS PART XV: THE TALE OF TALOS

As the returning Argonauts passed Crete, they found their ship attacked by huge boulders, and they soon realized the cause: On the beach stood Talos, an enormous bronze giant, and he was hurling the rocks.

"I heard he is the last of the race of brazen men, living creatures of pure metal," said Pollux.
"Pollux! You are wrong. It's a machine shaped like a man, built to defend Crete from invaders by Hephaestus himself," said Castor, his brother.
"Whatever it is, we must defeat it, or we cannot pass," said Jason.

A small group of Argonauts swam stealthily to the beach to observe Talos. Talos paced up and down the beach in a seemingly random way: They saw him take nine large steps to a small pile of boulders he had made, lift one, then take two steps and hurl it in the direction of the *Argo*.

"If he is a living being, I can drive him into madness with a concoction of my own," said Medea. "I need but pour it in his ear."

Talos now took seven steps closer to the water to see if his boulder had hit the ship. Then he walked four steps toward a tree that grew on the beach.

"If it is an automaton, your poison will do nothing but lubricate its mechanisms!" said Castor. "I see that it has a long vein running up its body, secured by a nail. If we remove that, perhaps the fuel that drives it will be released, and it will stop working."

Talos ripped the tree up from its roots and, taking five steps, threw it like a javelin toward the ship! As the tree struck the *Argo,* damaging its side, Talos took six steps backwards, either to enjoy its success or simply to get another boulder. Jason was unsure.

"If he is alive, pulling the nail out might simply enrage him further," said Medea. "What say you, Jason – is he man or machine?"

Jason knew that if Talos was alive, his actions need not make logical sense, whereas if it was a machine, its actions would follow some kind of pattern.

 Question: Is Talos a man or a machine, and how do you know?

PELOPS' PROGRESS

After they brought him back to life, Tantalus' son Pelops became strangely beloved of many of the gods of Olympus, especially Poseidon. They considered that since Pelops had been reborn through magic, he was no longer a mere mortal, especially as he now had an ivory shoulder made by Hephaestus. Poseidon taught him how to ride the divine chariot, and they would engage in many races.

In fact, it was one such race that caused him to be expelled from Olympus. The gods had been drinking and decided to race each other, 12 laps of the course, with the rule that all their chariots would be the same, all their horses the same, and they would not use any of their divine gifts to cheat.

On the oval chariot track, they all waited in their chariots at the single starting line: Zeus, Poseidon, Artemis and Pelops. At the correct moment, Hera raised the traditional bronze eagle and the charioteers surged out of the gates! They were all equally matched, and in fact equally drunk. But at the end, despite having no special skills, Pelops beat the other chariots quite handily. It was at this point that Zeus began asking questions about this young upstart and, realizing he was Tantalus' son, threw him off the mountain.

 Question: If all the chariots were equal, the horses equal and the drivers of equal skill, why did Pelops so easily beat the other three charioteers?

TARQUIN'S HAT

Before Lucius Tarquinius Priscus became the fifth King of Rome, he had faced challenges in his political success. He had inherited his father's fortune but was barred from holding any official role in Tarquinii because of his father's Corinthian heritage.

Tanaquil, his wife, suggested they move to Rome, where he might find more advantage. As they drew nearer, they knew Rome must be close, as they saw a statue of the she-wolf who had suckled Romulus and Remus, the twins whose legend led to the founding of Rome. In fact, Tarquin had worn a hat made of the finest wolf-cub skin in the hope that the Romans would take it as a sign of respect.

As they rode further, suddenly an eagle swooped at Tarquin and in one swift move grabbed his hat in its talons and took it away. It circled for a moment, screeching, and began flying away from them before suddenly reversing its course and placing the hat back on his head, then flying away!

Tarquin was stunned. His wife offered an explanation:

"You shall become king of Rome! The eagle is the symbol of Jupiter; it came from the sky, which is his realm; and it touched your head, the noblest part of a man – and where a crown sits!"

Tarquin was happy to accept this prognostication. However, even though it turned out to be true, there was another possible, if no less ridiculous, explanation for these events.

 Question: Why else might the eagle have stolen and then replaced Tarquin's hat?

THE COUNTERFEIT COIN

A Roman shopkeeper, Gaius, once called a friend of his into his taverna.

"I have a... quandary, Septimus. Do you see these five coins?"

Gaius spread out five golden Aureas. This was during the height of the empire's power, and they would, or should, all be pure gold.

"I was just given these in payment for some of my finest cloth. And the man who bought them... was Mercury."

Septimus briefly thought to scoff at the idea that his friend had met the god of messengers, but the serious expression on his sober friend's face stopped it in his throat.

"Well, this is a great blessing for you!" Septimus exclaimed. "Mercury is the god of commerce!"

"He is also the god of theft and trickery," said Gaius. "Don't misunderstand me, he is wise and beneficent," he added swiftly so as not to anger Mercury.

Gaius explained his interaction. Mercury had cast the five coins – much more than the cloth was worth – in front of him. But then Mercury counselled him that he was not to boast of possessing "the gold of Mercury," and so one of the coins was in fact counterfeit – not gold at all! If he spent that one by accident, a terrible curse would fall upon his entire family!

"Ah, this should be easy. Let me get my scales," said Septimus. But Gaius held up his hand.

"It would not work. Mercury told me he had enchanted the coin not only to look exactly like gold but also to weigh exactly the same, even though the coin is mere copper. Scales will not help."

Septimus laughed. "Did he say he had made any other enchantments?"

"No, that's it."

"Well then, my friend, to find it is even easier. Anyone could do it, unless they were a newborn babe."

 Question: What's the quickest, easiest way to find the fake coin?

A FLAMING TRICKY PUZZLE

In his youth, Achilles was raised by the Centaur Chiron. He taught his young charge everything from astrology to combat, from playing the lyre to the taxonomy of the creatures and monsters that dwelt in the world.

Achilles was particularly fascinated by the phoenix, the magical bird that, when it reached a great age, would burst into flame and, from the ashes, be born anew.

"Is the phoenix immortal, then?" Achilles asked with enthusiasm.
"No, child," Chiron answered. "Only the gods are immortal, and even they may die on occasion. The phoenix can only renew itself so many times, but it is indeed probably the most long-lived creature on earth. There's a riddle that can tell us its age, but I will leave out the animal names to make it more challenging:

"A chattering 1 lives now nine generations of aged 2,
but a 3's life is four times a 1's,
and a 4's life makes three 3s old,
while the 5 outlives nine 4s.

"The animals, my child, are a phoenix, a man, a stag, a crow and a raven –
but not in that order."

 Question: If Chiron tells Achilles that a raven lives 102 times the lifespan of number 2, and that the phoenix has 25 ½ times the lifespan of a stag, which number matches which animal?

WHERE'S SPARTACUS?

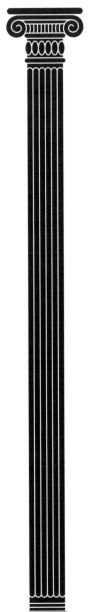

During the Third Servile War – the major slave uprising against the Roman empire – one man stood out among the leaders of the revolution: the former gladiator known as Spartacus.

One legend tells of how, when Spartacus and many of his men were captured after a disastrous battle, the Romans sought to locate Spartacus to give him a particularly harsh punishment. As the story goes, the Romans threatened to execute everyone unless Spartacus stood forward. But before he could do so, every man there declared himself to be Spartacus. This condemned them all to death, but showed their loyalty and dedication to him and their cause.

The truth was somewhat stranger. In real life, Spartacus was not an idealistic preacher but a pragmatic man, enslaved for desertion from the army, and all his men were not asked to identify him. Instead, the Romans captured six men who declared their names to be Artacus, Bartacus, Cartacus, Dartacus, Eartacus and Felix.

"Tell us – which of you is Spartacus?" the general shouted.
"Sir, they have sworn by all the gods that they will each only speak once, and that Spartacus will tell the truth and the others will lie. They say a master of logic like yourself must easily be able to find Spartacus this way, or else it would be honourable to release them all."
The general stroked his chin. "Very well... speak."
Artacus said, "Bartacus is Spartacus!"
Bartacus said, "Dartacus will tell the truth!"
Cartacus said, "Eartacus and Bartacus are liars."
Dartacus said, "Cartacus is lying!"
Eartacus said, "Bartacus is Spartacus."
And Felix said, "I am Spartacus!"

 Question: Who is Spartacus?

THE SIX LABOURS
OF THESEUS

Less well known than Hercules' 12 labours, Theseus' labours happened when he dug up his absent father's sandal and sword, and left to travel and meet him, deliberately choosing the more difficult land path rather than going by sea. His mother used her powers of sight to tell him that he would pass six entrances to the Underworld, each guarded by a particular chthonic bandit who menaced and attacked locals. He would have to defeat each with his skill and wit.

THE FIRST LABOUR:
THE CLUB OF PERIPHETES

His first challenge was outside the entrance that lay in Epidaurus.

Theseus had advance warning of the bandit here, known as Periphetes. A child of Hephaestus, like his father he needed a stick to walk. But as he ambled up to wanderers, they did not realize that his walking cane was also a hefty bronze club, and as soon as they came within his range he would swing it in the air, knock them onto the ground with a flurry of precise blows, and rob them of their possessions.

As Theseus approached him, Periphetes hobbled in his direction with an innocent smile on his face, but Theseus held out his hand.

> *"Halt! I know of thee, Periphetes the club-bearer. The legend of your clubbing abilities has not escaped me. You cannot surprise me, and yet I suspect you will not simply let me pass, so I propose a contest."*

Theseus suggested that they stand two sticks in the ground; then each could take a turn pounding their stick into the ground, and the one who used the fewest blows would be the winner.

Periphetes went first. He raised his club over his head and *WHACK!* He knocked the stick all the way into the ground in a single blow.

He turned and smiled smugly at Theseus, who held out his hand for the club.

> *"But you cannot win!" said Periphetes with confusion and anger.*
> *"Can't I?" said Theseus, and Periphetes reluctantly handed him the club.*

Sure enough, Theseus ended up walking away as the victor, having used two blows!

 Question: How did Theseus win?

THE SECOND LABOUR:
SINIS THE TREE-SPLITTER

At the Isthmus of Corinth lay the second entrance and the second robber. Sinis was notorious for asking explorers if they would help him with two pine trees that he had tied down. While they were holding one of them, he would quickly lash their hand to it, then to the second, and then, releasing both trees, he would tear the people in half!

Luckily Theseus had also received warning of Sinis' trick and undertook to beat him at his own game. Unfortunately, he decided to do this by trying to pull Sinis' exact trick on him.

And so Sinis was returning to his lair when he chanced upon Theseus with two tied-down pine trees near a sheer cliff face. He was so baffled and amused by someone clearly trying the same trick on him that he decided to play along for a moment.

As he was helping Theseus with the first tree, he allowed him to tie his hand to it. Sinis had a concealed dagger in his belt, and as soon as Theseus tried to tie his second hand, he would stab him in the chest!

As Theseus reached over, Sinis readied himself. But Theseus spotted the dagger and quickly moved out of range.

"You fool!" Sinis hissed. "Did you really think you could gull me with my own trick? I'll never let you tie my second hand!"

A minute later, Sinis was dead, most of the bones in his body shattered. And yet he was right: Theseus could not tie his second hand.

 Question: How did Sinis die?

THE THIRD LABOUR: THE CROMMYONIAN SOW

The third menace roamed near the village of Crommyon, and was not a human at all, but an immense sow taken to attacking people in the area at night, although recently there had been fewer assaults.

Theseus had heard that a wise woman and seer lived in the woods and might be able to give him knowledge about the beast.

"You must ensure her safety!" his mother told him.

But when he arrived at her house, he found that the door had been smashed outwards!

Entering the woman's dwelling, he saw that her furniture had been smashed and her clothes torn and strewn around the place. Her cupboards were also torn open, although they all seemed to contain only acorns.

He moved through the rooms, one of which seemed full of wet mud! In the farthest one, he found what seemed to be a wooden cage. It was broken, but it had strong wooden bars in a lattice.

Looking for signs of the beast, he found many hoof shapes in the mud on the floor, as well as human footprints (the woman?) and some strange kind of third footprints that didn't look exactly like that of a beast or a human, but something in between.

Leaving the house, he ventured further into the woods and saw the tracks and broken branches that indicated the creature's trail; soon enough he came across the monstrous sow, twice as large as a human, making its menacing way through the trees.

He notched an arrow. But then suddenly he paused and decided not to fire. Instead, he thought he might contact one of the gods and see if they would help.

 Question: Why does Theseus not shoot the sow?

THE FOURTH LABOUR: SCIRON

Near Megara, another robber would waylay wanderers and murder them in an unusual way.

Sciron would stop people who were moving along a path that ran along the south-facing cliffs of the area. He would hold them at knifepoint and force them to clean his feet. But he would be standing facing south near the edge, and as soon as they bent down and began cleaning, he would sharply kick them over the cliff and onto the sharpened rocks below! He'd descend at the end of the day to collect his prizes.

Luckily, Theseus once again knew that this is how Sciron would murder people. So when he walked along the path, he feigned ignorance, and when Sciron drew his dagger and ordered him to wash his feet he agreed to comply.

Then, as he was beginning to kneel, Theseus confused Sciron with a series of seemingly innocuous statements. First, he said that Sciron surely wouldn't want to be staring right at the sun as he washed his feet. Sciron agreed, and they turned. Then Theseus said that Sciron would probably want a pumice stone, and Sciron permitted him to grab one. Then Theseus said that the wind blowing from the east would be too harsh; Sciron agreed and they turned again.

Then Theseus asked if he could cover his face with a cloth to avoid the smell; Sciron agreed to that too.

Finally, Theseus knelt; but 10 seconds later, Theseus was not plummeting off the cliff. Instead, Sciron himself was dead.

 Question: Why couldn't Sciron kill Theseus with his usual trick?

THE FIFTH LABOUR: KING CERCYON

Unfortunately, Theseus was not warned about the fifth bandit. He stopped at a small taverna near the holy site of Eleusis and rested, before doing the usual ablutions that were customary at the time: Instead of washing with soap and water, Theseus covered himself in a mix of clay and ashes before dousing on a lot of olive oil. Before he could begin scraping the mix off with a strigil, one of the serving maids ran into the room.

"Sir, Cercyon is on the path... You said we should tell you..."

Without saying anything, Theseus threw on a loin cloth and leapt from the room and out of the building.

As he raced up the path, he could see an incredible, tall, musclebound man flexing and fixing Theseus with a manic glare.

King Cercyon's chosen pastime, you see, was to wrestle anyone who came along the path and, once he'd beaten them, kill them. Sort of like King Amycus, but with more full-body contact.

Nobody had ever defeated Cercyon because of his incredible physical strength, which exceeded even that of semi-divine heroes like Theseus. His preferred opening gambit was grabbing his opponent in a grappling clinch hold like a bear hug – and nine times out of 10 he could simply squeeze the life out of them!

In the end, Theseus defeated him with his superior skills, practically inventing the more skilful form of wrestling that the ancient Greeks preferred. But he would have been unable to do that if he had not survived the moment where Cercyon lunged forward and grabbed him in a bear hug!

 Question: If Theseus was not as strong as Cercyon, and Cercyon got him in a bear-hug hold at the beginning, why did it not crush him?

THE FINAL LABOUR: PROCRUSTES THE HOTELIER

His final challenge was the Underworld entrance on the plains of Eleusis. There dwelled the worst one of all – or so Theseus had heard. Procrustes the feared! The vicious! The... landlord of a small hostel where people could stay.

Theseus arrived at the rather well-maintained lodgings and was greeted at the door by Procrustes.

"Ah, well met, young sir! We happen to have a full complement of beds available if you would like to rest here tonight."

However, Theseus already knew Procrustes' little secret: He would deliberately give his guests a bed either too small or too big for them, and then "help" them by either stretching them to be taller or chopping off their feet or head if the bed was too short.

Theseus needed to make sure that whichever bed he ended up in would be exactly the right size for him, so that when night-time came Procrustes would be unable to act.

For that reason, he swiftly ran into the sleeping area and perused the beds. Theseus was 1.9m tall by modern standards.

Each of the beds was a different size, wildly varied, but all were half as wide as they were long. There was a 2m-long bed, a 1.7m-long bed, a tiny 0.5m-long bed, a giant 3.8m-long bed and a 1.8m-long bed.

Theseus made his choice, and that night Procrustes found Theseus sleeping sweetly, fitting perfectly on the bed.

 Question: Which bed did Theseus choose, and how did he fit on it?

THE CHALLENGE OF THE PALLANTIDES

Finally Theseus arrived at Athens to meet his father, King Aegeus. But tales of his deeds had preceded him. The 50 sons of Aegeus' younger brother Pallas, known as the Pallantides, decided to seperate into two groups and attack Theseus in a pincer movement. But Theseus and his men easily discovered both groups.

"I know you wish to fight me for the right to inherit my father's kingdom," Theseus said. "But you cannot all attack me at once – it wouldn't be fair."

The Pallantides admitted that it might be unfair, not quite realizing that Theseus meant he could easily kill all 50 of them himself.

"I suggest you choose one of you to face me in battle, and when... if I defeat him, you abandon your claim to the throne and support me instead. If one of you cannot fight me on his own, you forfeit."

The brothers discussed this and agreed in principle, but couldn't decide who should face him. They all considered themselves the greatest fighter in the group. In the end Theseus had another suggestion.

"It is simple. The direct heir would have the most to gain, so whoever amongst you has the earliest birth date must fight me. Swear to it now, on the gods."

The brothers all agreed that this was the fairest way, and swore to it. But then they suddenly realized that they had been tricked! None of them could fight Theseus, and they would indeed be forced to forfeit.

 Question: Why, based on the rules that Theseus laid out and the brothers agreed upon, is no-one able to fight him?

THE TRIBUTES

Now we come again to the labyrinth. King Minos, the owner of the labyrinth, had made a dark agreement with King Aegeus after his son was murdered at a sporting event hosted by the Athenians. In exchange for "peace," the Athenians had to choose seven young men and seven young women every year and send them to Crete as "tributes" to be put into the labyrinth, where the Minotaur would devour them.

After a couple of years, Theseus decided this could not continue. He would have to go to the labyrinth himself and see if he could somehow reason with the beast – or if not, then defeat it.

He disguised himself and replaced one of the tributes aboard the boat.

However, when it arrived at the port it seemed that somehow word had got out about Theseus' plan. So Minos' men decided to search the tributes to see if Theseus hid among them.

However, after searching the seven young men, they found no evidence of any of them being Theseus and decided the reports had been false.

 Question: How was Theseus able to avoid detection?

FINDING THE ENTRANCE

Theseus separated from the group to investigate the palace, which is how he met Ariadne and got the string, as well as a poisoned magical sword and a brooch that she said protected against bludgeoning.

> *"Wait, they have already taken the other tributes to the labyrinth!"*
> *Ariadne said, looking out the window. "You must hurry!"*
> *"Where is the entrance?"*
> *"That's the thing – finding the entrance is part of the*
> *challenge! The walls surrounding it seem unbroken,"*
> *said Ariadne. "All I know is, the key is three."*

Theseus didn't understand this, but set off toward the labyrinth and saw that it truly did seem to have no entrance. Then he saw three women sitting nearby, sewing. The Fates?

Perhaps this was the three.

> *"Tell me, ladies, where is the entrance to the labyrinth?"*
> *The first lady said, "I know you! If you must interfere, please go."*
> *The second lady said, "Go to east, then west, find half of three."*
> *The third lady said, "Words like vines! Broken vases and rotten*
> *mountains climb!"*

At first Theseus didn't understand at all. But then he realized the truth.

 Question: How did Theseus figure out how to get into the labyrinth?

RIDDLE OF THE MINOTAUR

Finally, Theseus found the middle of the labyrinth. He could see in the gloom a huge, looming figure, its breath deep and loud. It lurched forward and knocked him unconscious in an instant!

When he awoke, he found the creature going through all his possessions: the string, his magical sword, his protective brooch, his sandals. When it saw Theseus was awake, it stared at him with eyes that seemed almost human.

"You came to kill me?"
"No, to talk. To ask you…not to kill any more of these young people."
"But I have to feed. And it is all the meat I get. And besides…I enjoy it."
The Minotaur smiled, showing its huge teeth. "But I do not often get conversation. So here is my idea: I will tell you a riddle. If you get it wrong, I will crush all your bones."
"And if I get it right?"
"I will use the answer to kill you."
Theseus saw he had little alternative, so he nodded assent.
"Here's the riddle: Made of metal. Sharp at one end. If I stab you with it, you bleed. What is it?"

Theseus felt like it wasn't much of a riddle. But he had an idea. And when he gave his answer, the beast was unable to kill him.

 Question: What answer did Theseus give?

The Odyssey Part I:
Penelope's One-Hundred and Eight Suitors

Odysseus was one of the greatest warriors of his time and a key figure in the Trojan war. But he is more famous for what happened afterwards, as he tried to return home to his wife and son.

The story begins at his palace, where his frustrated wife, Penelope, had waited years for his return. In that time the house had filled with many young suitors trying to court her, but primarily just exploiting *xenia* to live there, eat all the food and basically enjoy luxury. There were 108 of them! However, they were still required to try to woo her while there, but were aware that if all 108 tried every day it would be intolerable. So they agreed that only one would woo her per day, and it would be chosen at random.

Every day the suitors would split into groups of 1-12 and a 12-sided die would be rolled. Whichever number came up meant the members of that group would be eligible to woo. They would then be numbered individually and roll the die again. If the individuals' number was rolled, they would woo Penelope. However, if none of their numbers came up, she would have a day off.

 Question: What is the percentage chance of Penelope having a day off?

THE ODYSSEY PART II:
CALYPSO'S ISLAND

Odysseus' son Telemachus worked with his mother to entreaty the gods to allow him to return home, as he had angered them. Poseidon would not relent; but in his absence, Zeus decided he would help.

The problem was that no-one was certain where Odysseus was. He had actually ended up shipwrecked on the island of Ogygia, the home of Calypso, a nymph and a daughter of Atlas.

Calypso had kept Odysseus captive there for seven years. The island was beautiful, and all his needs were met. Calypso loved him and wanted him to join her in immortality, but as time went on, he managed to break the hold of her magical singing, and began to ask more and more to return to his wife and family. Calypso hoped he would come around to her way of thinking, but eventually, one day, she confronted him in the gardens, bearing a gleaming spear.

"Odysseus, I ask you this one last time: Do you want to be immortal, or do you want to die?"

Odysseus considered this carefully and then answered.

Within the hour he had set sail on a raft that Zeus had provided for him.

 Question: What did Odysseus answer, and how was he able to leave the island?

THE ODYSSEY PART III: DON'T FORGET THE LOTUS

Eventually Odysseus' raft landed at Schere, the island of the Phaeacians. He dwelled with them for a few days, recovering, not telling them his name. But his reaction to a song about the Trojan Horse led them to realize his true identity, and he began telling them how he came to be on the island of Ogygia.

His men had set sail in 12 ships after the war, and all seemed well; but foul winds had led them to become becalmed for nine days, and when they landed, they feasted well on a strange flower with a blue middle and golden petals with vermilion edges.

Other people occupied the island too, in robes of magenta and apricot and saffron, with headpieces of crystal and cobalt. Their blue and brown and green eyes seemed unfocused and their smiles, though wide, were sloppy, and soon Odysseus' crew realized why. The flower they ate was a lotus that was so delicious, when you ate it you cared about nothing else – not the golden sands of your home, or the auburn hair of your wife, or the vivid red of blood drawn in battle. Only the flower. Odysseus hadn't eaten any of the lotus, so he had to physically drag each of his men back to the boats and lock them there until they had left the island and its strange powers of forgetfulness.

 Question: Without rereading the passage, can you say what shade the lotus was?

THE ODYSSEY PART IV:
SLEEPING CYCLOPS

Once his men had recovered, they sailed until they came to a lush, seemingly uninhabited island. They ventured inland until they found a cave to the west, filled with wine and meats and cheeses and, most importantly, no lotuses.

But of course, the island wasn't unoccupied; it was the home of the fearsome monocular Cyclopes, and the cave was the residence of their leader, Polyphemus. He sealed the east-facing entrance with an enormous boulder, and then proceeded to treat it as a larder, opening it and eating a couple of the crew before resealing. Polyphemus was cunning but in many other ways quite naive, happily tending his sheep during the day and then sleeping in the cave with Odysseus and his crew at night, sealing the entrance with the boulder and then lying down next to them, seemingly unafraid of them causing him any harm.

"Little men hurt me?" he scoffed. "Fleas bite dog, not kill dog."

But he had underestimated Odysseus' natural strength. And once Odysseus had eaten and drunk enough of Polyphemus' copious food supplies, he felt that he would have enough strength to kill the one-eyed giant by driving a sharpened spear deep into his eye!

"It must be a swift strike. I would suggest you all hold him down, but we are not as strong as him, even with all our brawn combined."

As he said this, suddenly Odysseus changed his mind.

"Actually, no. We shouldn't kill him in his sleep. We must find another way."

Question: Why should Odysseus and his men not kill Polyphemus as he sleeps?

THE ODYSSEY PART V: OL' ONE EYE IS BACK

Odysseus pondered the situation for a while, keeping the Cyclops from eating more of his men by getting drunk with him. When Polyphemus asked Odysseus his name, he lied and said, *"Nobody."*

"Tough to be nobody," Polyphemus said. "I'm somebody. All Cyclopes do what I say. I'm important. Nobody tell Cyclopes what to do except me and the gods."

Odysseus had an idea. He waited until Polyphemus passed and stabbed his eye with the sharpened stake – not to kill but instead to wound. He hoped the other Cyclopes would pull the boulder away when they heard Polyphemus' cries of distress, but when Polyphemus shouted, "Nobody has attacked me!" his brethren assumed his pain was some kind of act of the gods and stayed away from his cave.

In the morning, as the sun rose, Polyphemus recovered slightly, not totally blind but very wounded, his eye much more sensitive to light. But his sense of smell and hearing were still incredibly acute. He now rolled the boulder away himself, peering out of the cave to see if he could summon his fellow Cyclopes. Odysseus and his men positioned themselves around him, one behind, one in front and one on either side. One of them would have to lead the attack on Polyphemus before he could get help.

 Question: Which of the four men has the best chance of attacking Polyphemus?

THE ODYSSEY PART VI:
THE OLD WINDBAG

After they escaped Polyphemus' island, Odysseus' crew found sailing difficult. After offering a tribute to Aeolus, ruler of the winds, Odysseus received a gift.

"This bag contains all four winds of the sea: north, east, south and west. They are held in place within, as they are held in place upon a map," said Aeolus. "As long as they remain within, your sailing will be smooth and unimpeded by any storms."

The original tale says that Odysseus, after peering in the bag, did not inform the crew of the true nature of the bag's contents, but instead kept it secret and apart from them. They coveted it, thinking it was treasure, and when he slept, they opened it and all the winds escaped, bringing storms upon them and practically sinking the ship.

What is not widely reported is that in truth one of the winds, the north, had already escaped before the crew had come anywhere near the bag, and therefore they were already doomed before they even made their mistake.

 Question: Why, of all the winds, had the north escaped?

THE ODYSSEY PART VII:
SIREN SIGNS

Because of their erratic course, the crew could not avoid the island of the Sirens. Luckily, they had anticipated this, and they all put beeswax into their ears, except for Odysseus.

"I need to hear their song," he said. "I have heard tell that those who hear their songs can learn truths, provided they survive."

The crew agreed to lash him to the mast, and not release him, no matter how much he begged or threatened them.

Once he was secured, they sailed near the island, and through the mists came two eerily beautiful voices, tempting, controlling his desires. He thrashed against the ropes, pleading desperately with the sailors and then swearing oaths of furious vengeance if they didn't untie him that second!

But they stood firm, tightening the ropes, and through the mists they finally saw the Sirens. They were out on a small beach at the edge of their island, with an enormous tumbling waterfall to the east churning out water with an almost deafening roar, and a dense, jungle-like forest to the west teeming with strange creatures.

There were three of them, sitting on three particular carved stones that they could see had some kind of musical symbols upon them. One sat on the central stone plucking a lyre as she belted out the hypnotic tune; one sat on the western stone and was beating some kind of enormous drum as she emitted a piercing counterpoint; and the third was not singing at all, but seemed to be trying to do some kind of alluring interpretive dance instead, although her eyes registered a kind of mute fury that suggested this wasn't what she wanted to be doing.

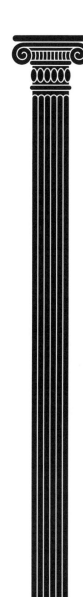

They made it past the island and eventually the sailors unplugged their ears and brought Odysseus down.

"Did you learn any truths?" his first mate asked.
"I learned something very important," he
said, but would not elaborate.
"Did you learn why the third one wasn't singing?" asked his friend.
"Not exactly, but I think I know anyway," he said.

 Question: Why wasn't the third Siren singing?

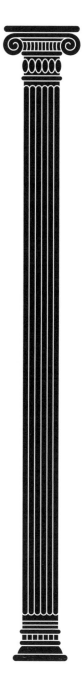

The Odyssey Part VIII:
Steer Clear

Having only just survived their encounter with the Sirens, and the aforementioned issues with Circe, Odysseus and his remaining men decided to try to be more cautious.

They found themselves at a port beyond which nothing could be seen, and concluded that they had reached the western edge of the world. There, Odysseus performed a *nekyia* ritual, sacrificing to the dead to summon the ghost of the legendary prophet Tiresias.

> *"Listen closely, Odysseus," said the ghost, almost transparently pale in thin, ashen robes, his wispy long beard blowing in some unseen spectral wind. "Set sail from here and you shall return home, and escape the interventions of Poseidon: churning oceans, rumbling earthquakes, enormous tempests, and... horses."*
>
> *"Great!" said Odysseus.*
>
> *"If you can," continued Tiresias, "avoid one thing: You must not steal the cattle from the island of Thrinacia. They are owned by Helios, god of the sun, rider of the golden chariot, lord of sight and sacred oaths."*
>
> *"OK. Don't steal Helios' cows. Understood."*

They set off, and as they came close to the island of Thrinacia, Odysseus insisted that they keep their distance. But the crew were hungry and thirsty, and so ended up landing there anyway.

"OK, go and find food, but if you encounter any cattle do not eat them," he said.

His men ventured further into the island and came across a large number of cows grazing in a field. A herder sat nearby mounted on a large steed, his three-pointed crook strangely mottled, his dark beard covering his face like a cloud.

"Uh... are these Helios' cattle?" a sailor asked.
"Nay," came the shepherd's rumbling voice, casting a spray
of saliva across their faces. "They are native to this land; I
watch over them only. Eat your fill, starving men."

And so they did – and obviously it turned out that they were Helios' cattle. They had been misled.

 Question: Who is the herder who led them astray?

THE ODYSSEY PART IX:
ODYSSEUS, MASTER OF DISGUISE

"And that is why what remained of my crew were shipwrecked by a vengeful Helios and Poseidon, and I ended up on Calypso's island," concluded Odysseus to a riveted audience of Phaeacians.

They agreed to help him return to his home, and transported him in his sleep to a dock near his house. There he met Telemachus and, with the help of the goddess Athena, disguised himself as a simple beggar so he could infiltrate his house without being blocked by the 108 suitors.

As he approached the home he had been absent from for many years, he found that much had changed. He could not enter or even see into the courtyard of the building without going through a hut that he remembered belonged to Eumaeus, his swineherd and former slave. He knocked erratically.

"Excuse me, young fella. I hope I'm not intruding, but me old legs are very weary, and I saw the blue tiles of your roof and although I know nothing of your household, I thought this looked like a place of kindness and generosity," Odysseus said in a creaky voice.
"Come inside, old man. This place is not as kind as it was, but I can find a crust of bread for someone such as yourself," said Eumaeus.

Odysseus toddled in and sat down slowly.
"Oh no, I don't need any food, although a sip of water from your
courtyard's clean well would slake my old thirst!" he said.
Eumaeus fetched him the water and sat with him as he gulped it down.
"Ahhh. Thank ye. Is your master a cruel man, then? I saw your light
on and it was like a beacon of provenance in this cold land."
"My master was kind and generous, but he has been lost
for 20 years, and in his place are parasitic jackanapes,"
said Eumaeus, explaining about the suitors.

Odysseus thanked his servant and, once he was asleep, slipped further into the house, touched that his swineherd would speak so kindly about him. What he didn't realize was that he had made an error that had meant Eumaeus knew it was not his first visit to the house, and had figured out his true identity.

 Question: How did Eumaeus know the old beggar was not a stranger to the house?

THE ODYSSEY PART X:
ODYSSEUS KILLS THE ONE HUNDRED AND EIGHT SUITORS

Still in his disguise, Odysseus entered the household and, although treated with disdain and disgust by the suitors, was greeted and welcomed in by Penelope. However, her warmth dissipated when he announced his intention to become her suitor as well. Throwing her hands up in frustration, she proposed a contest where whichever suitor could shoot an arrow through 12 axe heads could have her hand.

Needless to say, Odysseus won this contest. In fact, none of the 108 suitors could even string a bow. But they were sore losers, and prepared to kill the "beggar" after he won, even though his incredible feat made Penelope realize his true identity.

Odysseus threw off his disguise and the suitors all gasped, although some of them gasped slightly later than the others because it took them longer to recognize him. He angled his bow at that and managed to slay 20 before they could even react. The remaining suitors quickly dashed in all directions away from the courtyard to hide all over the house.

"You'd best hunt them down, my love," Penelope said.
"I have waited 20 years to return home," Odysseus said. "I will not spend hours chasing rats out of it. I have learned something during my journey that will bring them all back here, where I can finish them off quickly."

Before Penelope could say anything, Odysseus opened his mouth wide. And shortly after he had finished, all of the suitors had quickly returned to the room for him to vanquish in battle.

 Question: How did Odysseus bring them back to the courtyard?

PSYCHOPOMP, QU'EST-CE QUE C'EST?

The rivers Acheron and Styx are the means by which those who have been given burial rites can be taken to the land of the dead in the Underworld. And the manner by which they make this journey is on the ferry of Hades' personal psychopomp (one who guides the dead to the afterlife).

Charon the ferryman is a mysterious figure whose own thoughts and desires are shrouded. Some accounts say he is ragged and vicious-looking, while others depict him as a dignified figure or a cloaked skeleton, like the reaper. But they all agree that you must pay the ferryman for your journey or be forced to wander the shores of the Styx for 100 years before being able to cross.

While some thought it was enough to bury the deceased with money or other valuable trinkets, in truth the only way to pay was with two coins placed on the dead person's eyes.

Many poor people were unable to do this, and were doomed unfairly to wander. But there was a wealthy tribe who were never able to pay. Despite using their incredible size and strength to rob and kill anyone unfortunate enough to chance upon their island, upon their death the members of this tribe would always come up short on the payment, even though they had many thousands of coins of all shapes and sizes.

 Question: What is this tribe, and why can't they pay the full fee to Charon?

CROSSING THE RIVER LETHE

The river Lethe flowed through the Underworld too, but its power was that of forgetting. Anyone who swam in the waters of the Lethe was destined to lose some of their memories.

Aeneas, the Trojan warrior, went on a search for a new homeland for his people and was resolved to consult the ghost of his father, (known as a shade in Greek mythology), so he knew he had to descend into the Underworld. As instructed by Deiphobe the Sibyl, he gathered a golden bough from a tree to give as a gift to Proserpina, the wife of Pluto.

In the Underworld, Aeneas faced many challenges, aided only by the Sibyl, who was surprisingly spry for a 700-year-old woman. As they journeyed through the depths, they were able to get a ride on Charon's boat by showing the bough. But a lost soul jostled the vessel and Aeneas dropped it in the river!

After much searching, the golden bough had somehow come to rest on the far shores of the Lethe.

"I must retrieve the bough. Perhaps I can cross that bridge," Aeneas suggested, pointing to an ornate crossing further up, partially obscured by the gnarled, bare limbs of the local trees.
"Nay, that is guarded by Cerberus, and he only lets people pass from the left bank to the right, not vice versa," said the Sibyl, touching her golden brooch thoughtfully.

So Aeneas jumped in and swam the eight yards across the river. When he reached the left bank, he had been so fast that he lost only one memory. Unfortunately, it was

the memory of having to retrieve the golden bough. He dutifully walked over the bridge past Cerberus and returned to the Sibyl empty-handed.

"Why did I go over there again?" he asked.

After a couple more attempts, they found that whatever they did, Aeneas would always forget he had to get the golden bough once he reached the left bank, and then cross over the bridge to the right bank. The rushing water of the Lethe made it impossible for Aeneas to hear the Sibyl from the right bank, even if she shouted.

 Question: How can Aeneas ensure he can swim across the Lethe and retrieve the golden bough successfully?

OUROBOROS

In the heart of Egypt, at the time of its status as a province of Rome, certain magical traditions thrived. Historical papyri that describe a variety of rituals, incantations and even spells show a Hellenized version of the original Egyptian beliefs, especially in regard to the cycle of death and rebirth symbolized by Ouroboros, the snake swallowing its own tail.

The immortality that this creature indicates was different to the supposed invulnerability of the gods, or even the magical immunity of heroes like Achilles. This was more akin to someone who, by sheer magical skill and will, had removed themselves from the circle of life and rebirth itself to become their own sacred circle of persistence.

One such "sorcerer" was Hermes Trismegistus. While his name indicated that he was viewed as a combination of Hermes and Thoth, the supposed author of the famous *Hermetica* was once a mortal man.

This legendarily wise priest king had apparently elevated himself to the level of a god through his magical spells and potions. The discussions of astrology and alchemy in his works were impressive, but any details of how he actually achieved this were, if ever recorded, lost to time.

What we do now know is that he was not truly immortal, as he was killed by one of his own students. Despite his many magical protections, he was murdered with a single act.

The student would not reveal how he did it. He would only say, "He claimed to be thrice great, but when the snake eats its own tail, three and three become six."

He claimed that the mind of Hermes Trismegistus was mortal. But we must remember that the Greeks did not consider the brain to be the seat of intelligence when we attempt to learn where he stabbed him.

 Question: Using the symbol of the Ouroboros, how did Hermes Trismegistus' student kill him?

HERCULES AND CACUS

During his tenth labour, after he had just stolen Geryon's cattle, Hercules had been forced to stop somewhere for the night with the cattle and rest them before he could continue moving them to the kingdom of Mycenae to give to King Eurystheus.

But as he slept, Hercules did not realize he was near the cave of the creature Cacus, a notorious cannibalistic monster.

Cacus emerged and considered attacking Hercules, but unlike many other monsters he was able to recognize the hero and knew it was a battle he could not win. But he did decide to help himself to three of the cows. However, Cacus realized that Hercules would be able to see where they had been led from their hoofprints! Thinking fast, he decided to line them up in a row and walk them backward into the cave instead. As they were near the river, Hercules would hopefully think that the cattle had run off in that direction and been swept away by the water. And they were camped close enough to the cave that hopefully Hercules would not notice that the hoofprints "started" near the cave's mouth.

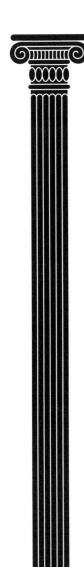

When Hercules awoke, he noticed the missing cows. He looked at the placid-looking remaining herd, at the wind blowing in from the east, at the hoofprints in the ground and the cowpats on the ground, at the sun rising in the distance, and at the cave mouth. And despite the hoofprints looking like they were going in the opposite direction to the cave, he knew what had happened.

 Question: How could Hercules tell what Cacus had done?

Knot a Good Idea

The tale of the Gordian Knot is often used as an example of how Alexander the Great's lateral thinking enabled him to lead his forces to conquer almost half the world and found one of the biggest empires in history. But even this iconic story has elements that have been disputed.

Gordium was the capital city of Phrygia.

Phrygian legend said that centuries ago the city was without a king, so an oracle declared that the next person to enter the city would become king. A simple ox-cart driver named Gordias arrived and was immediately crowned! In tribute to him, the ox-cart remained in the palace secured very tightly to a post with a fiendish knot made up of several different kinds, bound so tightly together it was all but impossible to discern their solution. The ropes were so tense that the cart itself almost seemed to vibrate with power, the linchpin rattling in the yoke.

When Alexander arrived in the city, Phrygia was a mere satrapy, or province of the Persian Empire, and there were once again no kings. But a new legend declared that whoever could untie the Gordian Knot was destined to rule, not just over the Phrygians but all of Asia.

Alexander could not resist the opportunity to solve this riddle. And the most famous explanation is that he drew his sword and severed it with a single swipe, demonstrating not only his intelligence but his ruthlessness as well.

But what if Alexander had chosen not to use his sword? He was a warrior, but he also understood diplomacy and the power of legend. If he had slashed it, would it have been disrespectful? Same if he burned it or dissolved it with something acidic. So there is an alternative answer for how he solved the puzzle.

 Question: How could Alexander solve the Gordian Knot without cutting it with his sword or any other sharp object?

Androcles and the Lion and Four Other Guys

The tale of Androcles (Androclus in the original Latin) speaks of a runaway slave who escaped his supposed master, a consul in a part of Africa then controlled by the Roman empire.

Androcles ran out into the wilderness and was forced to take shelter in a cave. As he entered, he suddenly heard a strange, echoing howl, and deeper within he found a lion lying on the ground snarling and whimpering. He noticed it was holding its paw strangely, and when he cautiously looked closer, he could see that it had a large thorn stuck in its paw.

Torn between compassion and fear, Androcles ultimately decided to carefully extract the thorn. The beast stood quickly, and after a moment swept out of the cave and beyond his sight.

Years later, Androcles was recaptured and sent to Rome to be punished for his escape. He was taken to the Circus Maximus, where he would be part of a group of slaves who would be mauled by wild animals for the sick amusement of the crowd.

Androcles was part of a group of five former escapees. He stood at the front of the line. Behind him was Antonius, a bitter man from Megara. Behind Antonius was Septus, who was terrified; and in the fourth and fifth positions were two brothers, Simonus and Treva, both Corinthians and fierce combatants. Antonius refused to be anywhere near them, as Megarans and Corinthians hated each other.

"Listen, Septus," said Simonus. "Let me go before
you. I cannot wait to face this beast."
"Yes, of course!" said Septus tremulously, swapping places
with Simonus. "I did not know we were permitted to move.
In fact, can I change places with you, too, Treva?"
"Why not?!" said Treva boldly. "I do not
care." And they swapped as well.
"Now I need to move," said Antonius. "I like not the smell
of the man next to me." And he swapped with one man.

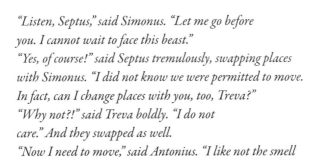

The gate was opened, and the crowd roared as they saw the first slave enter the arena. There stood the lion, the same lion whose injury was soothed by Androcles. It hesitated as it saw the man who had entered... and then jumped onto him, savagely tearing him to shreds!

 Question: If we accept that the lion is the same one, and that it is able to recognize Androcles, why did it attack?

TAKING THE PYTHIA

As is evident in our tales so far, the role of oracles, and their predictions in the culture and mythology of Ancient Greece, was significant. Many of their leaders and ordinary people relied on their predictions, whether it was to make big decisions or avoid tragic outcomes. However, the role that fate plays in these interactions means that anyone who seeks to avoid the consequences of a truthful prediction will always fail, and in some cases ultimately cause the thing to happen in the first place!

Despite this, the ability of oracles to tell the truth without consequences was not always guaranteed, as while people often respected their insight, they could also become enraged by the sad nature of their prophecies.

The most famed oracle was the Pythia, who lived at the temple in Delphi. This was a large community of oracles and priests, and the Pythia proved herself to be the most accurate oracle in the land when she correctly predicted what Croesus, ruler of the vast kingdom of Lydia, was eating on a certain day. So when he sought her counsel on the wisdom of going to war with the Persian Empire, he was delighted to hear that if he went to war with the Persians, he would destroy a mighty empire.

After the cataclysmic failure of his campaign and the defeat of his army, a ragged, scarred Croesus returned to Delphi and held the Pythia and her attendants at sword-point.

"Your prediction... was wrong," he hissed.
"Sadly, it wasn't," she said.

 Question: How was the Pythia's prediction correct?

PYTHIA

THE SKILLS OF PIRITHOUS

Not every "hero" in mythology was as incredibly skilled as men like Hercules or Perseus. In fact, Theseus' best friend, Pirithous, while a capable warrior in many ways, did not match his comrade's incredible abilities. He was somewhat decent with a sword and could act with great stealth (as demonstrated when he rustled cattle away from Theseus as a prank), but the one area he could never succeed in was archery.

Pirithous was notoriously bad with a bow and arrow, and if he ever picked one up everyone would immediately throw themselves behind any object or piece of furniture large enough to block an arrow from accidentally hitting them. After a while he became very frustrated by this and, despite constant training, never seemed to get any better.

One day Theseus saw his friend marching determinedly off into the woods with a bow, a handful of arrows and a small pot of red paint. Curious, he followed, and as he approached a small copse, he could hear the twang and thud of arrows being fired and hitting a tree.

When he eventually found his friend, he saw something unexpected: On an enormous oak tree was drawn a large target of three concentric rings in red paint, and right in the middle of the middle ring were three arrows.

"What do you think, Theseus?" Pirithous said,
grinning as he picked up the bow.

"It's a rather large tree. And a rather large target," Theseus noted.

"I'll give you that. But I should say it still
deserves admiration!" Pirithous said.

"Where were you standing when you fired the arrows?
At arm's length?" said Theseus teasingly.

"No! I stood a good distance away!" Pirithous said. And Theseus had
to admit that the time between hearing the arrow loosed and hearing
it hit the tree did suggest that Pirithous had not done this at point-
blank range! Neither had he knocked these particular arrows in by
hand, as Theseus could see around the target the splintered pieces of
tree bark indicating an impact, glistening with specks of red paint.
Theseus looked briefly again at the shafts of the
arrows and then turned to his friend.

"Nice try, Pirithous," he said.

 **Question: How does Theseus know Pirithous did not achieve
three bullseyes with his archery skill?**

An Oracle Miracle

An oracle's greatest fear was not that their predictions would lead to woe and bloodshed (this was almost always the case), but that people would begin to doubt their oracular powers. Some oracles would rely on particularly vague pronouncements like, "You will come to misfortune," but then they would be criticized for not being helpful. In many cases, if an oracle was inaccurate, it didn't particularly matter, as the person who consulted them would often be too preoccupied with the fallout, or dead.

The oracle at Didyma prided herself on the specificity of her predictions, so it was a source of concern to her when the leader of the army arrived to execute her.

"Your predictions simply do not work. You said the enemy would come by sea, but they entered via the land. You said they would attack at night; they began their assault in the day. You said that rain would swamp the field and we should look to archers; but the sun baked the ground hard, and their ground forces were obscured by dust! Your predictions are worthless, meaningless."
"If she said birds could fly, I'd look for them tunnelling underground!" said a soldier next to him.
"Silence!" shouted the commander to the soldier. "Execute her now!"

The soldier raised his sword to strike her down, and she had to think fast.

Question: What can she say to save her life?

- If you kill me, you will not learn the secret of eternal life!
- Your sword blow is destined to miss!
- If you kill me, you will be cursed forever!
- If you kill me, you will have great success in the future!
- You cannot kill me, I am immortal!

NOT A WATERTIGHT SOLUTION

A small crew of notably strong and large hunters decided to travel down the Thermodon in a small but sturdy skiff to hunt a herd of silver-furred deer they had heard lived in the woods.

What they didn't realize was that at the mouth of the Thermodon lay Themiscyra, the home of the Amazons.

Suddenly a volley of arrows cascaded toward their boat, and they had no sooner held up their shields than a small group of Amazons appeared in a boat of their own behind them!

The hunters tried to throw off the Amazons' pursuit but found that they kept up with them at every twist and turn of the river. Their only hope was to direct their boat toward the whitewater rapids and hope that the Amazons' skiff would be damaged on the jagged rocks.

As they were buffeted by the sharp boulders, they were relieved to see that the Amazons' boat had been scraped and was beginning to take on water. Then they realized that their boat, too, had been holed and was beginning to fill!

The men saw that the Amazons were using their shields to bail the water out and began doing this themselves. There were six Amazons in their boat, and eight men in theirs. The men's shields were twice the size of the Amazons', and the men themselves each had a larger build than the Amazons as well. They began bailing only 30 seconds after the Amazons began, and the Amazons had been taking on water for at least two minutes before they started, whereas the men started bailing within 20 seconds of their vessel getting a hole!

And yet, despite their two boats being almost identical, the size of the holes being the same, and the men having a greater capacity to bail than the Amazons due to having larger, rounder shields, the women on the boat successfully cleared all the water out of their boat before the hunters could, and descended on them with raised spears.

 Question: Considering all the facts, why could the Amazons bail their boat out quicker than the men?

ARTEMIS AND ORION

A rtemis, the goddess of the wilderness and the hunt, spent years trying to find an equal in her abilities to act as her hunting companion, and it was Orion the giant who finally claimed that role. The two of them were firm friends and would often spend time in forests and on plains across the world pursuing and killing many of the beasts. They would travel between these places using Artemis' magical golden chariot, pulled by four deer with golden horns that could fly across the sky at incredible speeds.

But it was during one such flight that Artemis' chariot was suddenly struck by a cuckoo in flight and began to lose its magical abilities! Convinced that the bird had been sent by her vengeful "stepmother," Hera, Artemis realized she had to try and stabilize the chariot or it would crash into the ground, killing them both. But while she and Orion were the same weight, their weapons and belongings were not, so the chariot wasn't balanced! Both of them wore a helmet with breastplate and shin guards, and had a sword and shield at their side, and neither of them were willing to throw any overboard, as they were enchanted and extremely valuable.

- Artemis' helmet was twice as light as Orion's.
- Artemis' shield was the same weight as Orion's helmet.
- Artemis' sword weighed 2kg.
- Artemis' breastplate was twice as heavy as Orion's shield.
- Orion's shin guards were each half the weight of Artemis' sword.
- Orion's helmet weighed 2.5kg.
- Orion' sword was one and a half times the weight of Artemis'.

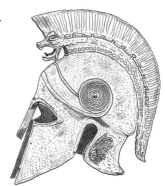

- Orion's lightweight shield weighed the same as one of Artemis' shin guards.
- Orion's breastplate was four times the weight of Artemis' sword.
- And Orion's shin guards were each half the weight of Artemis' helmet.

 Question: Considering the relative weights of their belongings and the fact that they are each on their side of the chariot and remain there, what would they have to exchange with each other to make the weight on both sides equal?

DEATH ON THE HALIACMON

No sooner had Hercules heard the strange wail from the pleasure boat than he mightily leapt over the river and onto its deck.

He saw a man lying dead, a crown wedged on his now severed head. Party guests stood by tables laden with food, looking horrified. An older woman wept uncontrollably in the arms of a court official.

"What has happened here?" asked Hercules, but everyone just stared at him fearfully. The man stepped forward.
"Mighty Hercules, I am Alcibiades, royal advisor."

Apparently, this was a celebratory dinner for the queen's birthday, with many guests, and a special golden baklava baked for the occasion.

"But I cannot say what happened next," said Alcibiades. He leaned forward and in a low whisper said, "The Kindly Ones."

Hercules understood. The Furies. Sometimes called the Kindly Ones to avoid upsetting them.

They were three female deities dedicated primarily to the death and punishment of men: Alecto punished those who acted in rage; Tisiphone killed men who sought disproportionate revenge; and Megaera was known to execute men for unreasonable jealousy.

The partygoers were too afraid to explain further. So Hercules looked around. The mess suggested that the Furies had made a surprise appearance and one of them had killed the man on the deck. Hercules would need to know which one, so he could inform the spirit of this river.

He looked at the body. The golden diadem seemed ill-fitting, almost wedged on. The hands and mouth were covered in golden flakes. Hercules looked around for the golden baklava and saw only a broken terracotta bowl on the deck.

He looked at the crying woman, noting her elaborate royal gown. A man standing next to her, a similar age to the man on the deck, darted forward.

"He brought it on himself! Father would be so disappointed... Such petulant disrespect."

He then saw that the woman was glaring at him and, with the chastised look of a little boy, stepped back once more. Hercules noticed that the young man also wore a diadem, but it was much less resplendent. He also noticed a similar one on the table.

"Of course!" Hercules exclaimed. "I have been the fool!"

 Question: Which of the Kindly Ones killed the man on the deck?

ROMAN WHISPERS

R omulus and Remus, the legendary twins whose exploits led to the foundation of Rome, were the grandsons of a deposed king (Numitor) and the grand-nephews of the man who deposed him (Amulius). They were raised in secret, away from the palace, by a family of shepherds, but grew up to be well-respected community leaders, and eventually suspicion of their true lineage led the supporters of Amulius to kidnap Remus and imprison him in the palace.

Romulus was determined to rescue his brother and knew there were some within the palace that still supported Numitor, so he sent a messenger to get information about how to break in and free his twin.

The messenger arrived with a look of confusion.

"I have the message, but I don't know if you can make sense of it."
The messenger paused, then said "Aat eexiit froont
noooon too. Aat blaack moooongaatee riight
stoop. Deesceend ceeiiliing froom looweer."
Romulus blinked. "What??"
"That's what I was told. It must be a code."

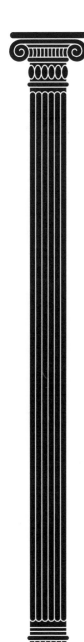

Romulus consulted with a former palace worker.

"I think I know what's happened," the worker said. "The three main conspirators against Amulius all have strange quirks in their writing, and I think this message must have passed through all three. The main source always says the opposite of things that have an opposite. The second doubles every vowel! And the third puts each sentence in alphabetical order."
"Of course, it makes perfect sense," said Romulus drily.

 Question: What is the actual message?

BAD VIBRATIONS

Orpheus, the musician who sailed with the Argonauts in our earlier puzzle, was the child of Apollo and the muse Calliope, and therefore his musical talent was superhuman. Thus, when he met Eurydice, he knew he had found his match. She was an Auloniad, one of the nymphs that live in wide, green areas like pastures, and her talent at dancing almost matched Orpheus' musical skills. She was so light-footed that she seemed to barely touch the ground as she danced.

They fell in love and quickly married, and many thought their union was perfect. But Hymen, the god of marriage, refused to bless them, saying he foresaw terrible consequences ahead.

Orpheus used to like to play his lyre in the meadows every morning.

"My love, do you not fear that a viper will attack
you as you play?" Eurydice asked.
"Snakes don't bother me," Orpheus responded. "All I need is to play these
little drums once in a while, and the good vibrations shake the snake, and
any python is py-gone in seconds! Vibrations give these slithers the shivers."

Taking his advice, Eurydice quite happily danced in the meadow, and even took to doing it on her own occasionally. And it was at this time that a viper darted out and bit her on the leg! She immediately died.

 Question: Why didn't Eurydice's dancing scare away the snake?

ORPHEUS PLAYS THE BLUES

Orpheus was so upset by his bride's death that he sat down and played the saddest lament that has ever been performed. It was so heart-wrenchingly pitiful that it felt like it made everyone in the world sad. And not just humans, but all supernatural creatures, and every one of the gods. Even the Furies wept. They even say that it made plants and inanimate objects tearful.

In truth, it was the music that had this incredible effect. Because, despite his playful manner of speaking, Orpheus didn't feel very confident in writing lyrics. He tried to express his true feelings in the words, but they came out very stilted and disjointed. Luckily, most of the world heard only his enchanted lyre and not the words he sang:

> *By viper's fang my life's been split,*
> *Thus, in darker tomb be hope quit,*
> *She fled to worlds under my sight...*

Then he found he could not think of another line. His friend Phocus arrived to offer his condolences.

"I can't figure out what the next line should be," Orpheus said. "It's all random."
"Orpheus, it is not random, and I know exactly
what your next line should be."

 Question: What should Orpheus' next line be, and why?

- **And now my heart is blackened grit.**
- **Sadly, our love is broken with it.**
- **On shadow wings my bird did flit.**
- **I'll find another, don't worry about it.**

COOL CATS

Orpheus' grief was so strong that he knew he had to travel into the Underworld to rescue Eurydice. He didn't have the strength of Hercules or Theseus, nor the godly powers of Demeter. But his song had touched the heart of the world, and the gods had decided that if he could enter the Underworld he would survive.

First he had to pass the twin guardians of the Underworld entrance at Cape Matapan. They were two Manticores, seemingly identical, their twitching scorpion tails dripping with venom as their enormous leonine faces scanned the area for any who dared to try and enter.

"If I play these cats a lullaby, they might fall asleep. But if they twitch their tails while they're snoozing, I might end up dead!" Orpheus said to Phocus as they crouched in the bushes watching the entrance.
"So they might sting you with their scorpion tails as they sleep?" asked Phocus.
"Well, could you make them dance out of the way?"
"Sure thing. I'll play a lively jitterbug that'll make these..."
"Just do it."

Orpheus emerged from the shrubbery and began playing a tune on his lyre, hopping from foot to foot in an imitation of Eurydice's nimble dancing. The left Manticore began to dance along with him, moving out of the way of the door. But the right Manticore sat still, staring ahead and not moving at all.

Phocus, confused, was suddenly granted a vision by the muse Calliope, Orpheus' mother, who told him four statements, three of which would help him understand.

 Question: Three of these statements are true and one is a lie. Which is which?

1. **Manticores do not like music.**
2. **The left Manticore cannot hear.**
3. **If Orpheus enters the Underworld, he will die.**
4. **The right Manticore cannot see.**

THE WALK

Orpheus entered the Underworld, and as he walked, he played. The shades – spirits of the dead – on the banks of the Styx swayed to the beat. Chthonic entities bobbed their heads. Even Cerberus began hopping around like a giddy puppy.

In the palace of Hades, the lord of the Underworld sat regarding Orpheus with an icy stare.

Orpheus began another lament, just for Hades. The lord began to weep. He waved his hand and Eurydice appeared, hypnotized.

"Why do you seek Eurydice?" he
asked grimly. "She dwells in Elysium. Can you offer better?"
"We're like Janus: two faces, same person," said Orpheus.
"You know everything about her?" Hades asked. "If you
think back, maybe there are details you missed..."
But Hades relented.
"Take her to the surface. She must walk directly behind you the entire way.
And if you turn to look at her at any point, she will remain here...forever."

Orpheus had to accept, so he turned around and began walking back, too anxious to play anything. The Underworld had gone quiet. Every shade, creature and chthonic god simply stared at him as he walked. Some of them clapped slowly or struck the ground, the sound echoing over the bubbling of the river. The further he got, the more a thought throbbed and grew in his mind: Why couldn't he hear any footsteps?

He knew that shades were insubstantial and wispy. But the Eurydice he saw was solid and real, exactly as in life.

Was this all some kind of cruel joke on him? But he kept his course.

As he approached the exit, he suddenly thought that if he left now, and she wasn't with him, he could never return!

He turned around in an instant…and had just enough time to see Eurydice before she was drawn swiftly back into the Underworld by a spectral wind that seconds later blew him out of the exit.

 Question: Why didn't Orpheus hear Eurydice?

How to Get Ahead in Music

Now in despair at his loss, Orpheus sought to return immediately to the Underworld. But since people who are alive can only visit once, he lost all interest in the mortal realm.

He wouldn't eat or drink, and simply began to waste away. But he couldn't die, as the gods and many other powers in the world desired his singing and music so much that they couldn't bear to be without it, in the same way that he couldn't bear to be without Eurydice.

So he played a final song designed to summon Thanatos himself, the personification of death, and convince him to take Orpheus' life. Thanatos was moved, and seconds later Orpheus was attacked by a pack of wild dogs, his spirit released to the Underworld to be with his love.

But strangely, Orpheus' musical gifts were so strong that his head somehow survived, and not only that, but it continued to sing. The songs it sang were still beautiful – although the words were meaningless syllables called glossolalia – and so achingly sad as to affect you forever. One of the Muses, the inspirational goddesses of arts, took Orpheus' head and kept it as a strange keepsake.

But which muse?

Calliope was Orpheus' mother. So she would have the greatest claim to it. But she was not the muse of music, but of epic poetry, considered at the time to be the greatest of the arts, as it combined storytelling with history and emotional resonance.

Melpomene was the muse of song, or at least she was once, and became the muse of tragedy, often depicted with the mask of tragedy in one hand and a knife in the other.

Euterpe was the muse of music. She was said to have invented many instruments, including the flute, with which she was often depicted. Later she became the muse of lyrical poetry, which she preferred due to her love of words and wordplay.

 Question: Which muse took Orpheus' head?

The Adventures of Atalanta
Part I: Centaurs of Attention

The legendary Greek heroine Atalanta was the fastest runner in the world. As a baby, she was deliberately abandoned on a freezing mountaintop because her father wanted a male child. A passing she-bear nursed her, and she was eventually adopted by hunters. She grew up admiring Artemis, the huntress goddess, and followed her example of asceticism and stealthy pursuit. But the one thing she could do better than anyone else was footracing, leaving anyone who tried to compete with her in the dust, and eschewing all vices.

She was also an excellent shot and could hit anything she aimed at with a normal, non-magical bow, whereas most heroes would rely on enchanted or blessed weapons.

One day Atalanta was hunting up in the mountains. She was not running at her full speed because the rocks underfoot were often loose and could crumble and start a chain reaction. Suddenly two Centaurs emerged from behind a tree line! Unlike the famous Chiron, these Centaurs were wild and aggressive, and were getting ready to attack Atalanta, their huge hooves carefully striding toward her.

As the mountain rocks were unsteady, if she turned and ran, she would not be able to achieve her top speed before they were upon her. She drew her bow but suddenly realized she had only one arrow! The Centaurs grinned nastily. Atalanta knew that she could only shoot one of them and that the other would immediately attack her, fearless and unconcerned about its fallen comrade. She had to think, and act, quickly.

 Question: Where should Atalanta shoot to escape the Centaurs?

Part II: Murder She Bowed

Atalanta's arrows were personally made for her by her fletcher, Jessica.

"One day I shall make an arrow that can fly faster than your fleetest pace,"
Jessica said as she carved some wood.
"If anyone can achieve this, it's you, my friend," Atalanta said kindly.

But suddenly they were both seized by brigands! These hunters from the forest had long been jealous of Atalanta's skill. They also resented that Jessica would only craft arrows for her friend and other women. So they had brought an enchantment that allowed them to move silently and sneak up on the women.

They tied Jessica to a tree, and then they marched Atalanta 100 feet away in a straight line.

"You think yourself the finest shot?" one of the hunters sneered. "Well, here is
your challenge."

One of the other hunters set up a target equidistant between Atalanta and Jessica, with a hole directly in the middle.

"You have one arrow, and if you score a bullseye directly
through the middle, we will release you and Jessica. We swear
on the gods," the hunter said with a mean smile.
"It is clear that when the arrow passes through the target it
will strike and kill my friend," said Atalanta solemnly.
"I don't think that will happen. Because I don't think you can make the shot,"
said the hunter. "But if you don't even try, we will kill you both anyway."
Atalanta thought. "Do you have any rules about
what I can do after I have fired the arrow?"
The hunter considered this. "No. It seems to me
that after that point, the die is cast."
"Then I accept your challenge," said Atalanta.

 **Question: How can Atalanta score a bullseye through the
target with the hole, and not kill Jessica?**

PART III: DON'T SPEAK

As Atalanta's fame grew, so did her list of enemies, from envious warriors and hunters to jealous gods. In particular Aphrodite resented her, because Atalanta spurned the idea of love or marriage. She had adventured for several months with Meleager, but despite his interest in her, she valued him primarily as a friend and gently spurned any advances.

The two of them were walking through a forest when they came across a strange, unfamiliar temple. Its courtyard was ringed by eight doors marked with Roman numerals, blocked by steel lattice gates. But as soon as they stepped inside, the door behind them slammed shut! And from each of the doors stepped monsters:

From Door I stepped one Manticore!
From Door II stepped two Centaurs!
From Door III flew three Harpies!
From Door IV stepped four Vrykolakas!
From Door V stepped five Ichthyocentaurs
(like Centaurs, but with fishes' tails)!
From Door VI stepped six Cyclopes!
From Door VII stepped seven Spartae!
And from Door VIII stepped eight Satyrs!

176

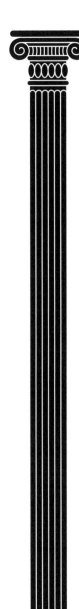

As the crowd of monsters began to surround them, Atalanta realized it must have been a trap from one of the gods – a trap for her specifically, as she noticed that they were circling her and seemed to be largely ignoring Meleager! She tried to shout to him but found a further issue: She couldn't speak!

As Atalanta began to use her speed and skill to fight the monsters, Meleager found a release mechanism for the doors, but it would take all his strength to open one, so they had to choose correctly. Luckily, Atalanta had noticed which door was an exit as the monsters had entered, but she couldn't speak, and if she took even a moment to point at it for Meleager's benefit she would be overwhelmed by the monsters!

Meleager watched as Atalanta dashed around the courtyard, but he noticed that she was dodging most of the creatures, only successfully killing a single Vrykolakas and two of the Ichthyocentaurs. Suddenly, he realized which door to open.

 Question: Which door must be opened, and how did Meleager know?

PART IV: BASILISK FAULTY

Atalanta realized that Aphrodite was behind the attacks. She needed to make a gift or sacrifice to the goddess to appease her – but without falling in love or marrying anyone. Artemis spoke to her, saying that Aphrodite had a beautiful temple on the island of Papho, reputed to be the sight of her birth. However, no-one could attend it, as it had become the home of three basilisks, horrible lizard creatures that could strike someone dead with a single gaze.

Aphrodite could not make them leave, as they were beloved of Cybele, the goddess of wild nature. So if Atalanta could kill them, Aphrodite might be extremely grateful.

Atalanta journeyed to the island and found that even though no-one could get past the basilisks, many had tried, driven by their dedication to Aphrodite. The ground was littered with corpses and skeletons. She knew that her only chance would be to kill them before they even saw her. She glimpsed all three silhouetted on the crest of a hill, as a young warrior charged them! He seemed to feint toward the left, but suddenly he clutched his chest and rolled down the hill, clattering over many bodies before falling conveniently next to where Atalanta was hidden.

"I...was wrong," he gasped. "One basilisk can see well, but another is blind in one eye, and the third cannot see at all! It is not evident from their appearance, but I thought by trial and error I had learned that the left basilisk was partially sighted, the middle was blind, and the right had full sight. I thought if I passed on the correct side of the left one, I had the best chance of survival. Now I realize I was wrong about every single one..."

And then he died. Atalanta noted that it had been the gaze of the left basilisk that had killed him. If she knew which basilisk was which, she could defeat them.

 Question: Out of the left, middle and right basilisks, which is blind, which is partially sighted, and which can see well?

PART V: THE THREE GOLDEN APPLES OF APHRODITE

Aphrodite was appeased by Atalanta's efforts and left her alone for a while. However, in the interim she joined the Argonauts on their quest and was integral in the defeat of the animal that killed Idmon, although that led to the death of her friend and admirer, Meleager.

News of this passed to her birth father, who arrived to claim her and quickly began trying to set her up in marriage.

Atalanta was still determined never to wed, so she got her father to agree to a stipulation: Any potential suitor had to defeat her in a footrace, and if they lost, they would be beheaded. By her. As her father was an arrogant man who disbelieved her abilities, he agreed happily. And as many of her suitors were similarly arrogant and disbelieving, there followed weeks of races and men being beheaded.

One man who believed in Atalanta's abilities was Hippomenes, one of the disciples of the Centaur Chiron. He was not so foolish to believe he could win against her without cheating. So he prayed to Aphrodite, who still bore a minor grudge and gave him a gift: three magical golden apples!

"When these are dropped, no-one can resist picking them up. Not even a certain fast-footed fan of Artemis," Aphrodite said softly.

And so, the legend tells that Hippomenes waited until the race began and then threw the apples to the ground, causing Atalanta to stop and pick them up, giving him the chance to get ahead of her.

But we know differently. Even with this trick, Atalanta's speed was much greater than Hippomenes'. In fact, Atalanta married Hippomenes because she found his failure endearingly bizarre and recognized that he saw her as a skilled runner and not just a conquest. So she threw the race – much better than how he threw the apples.

 Question: Why did the golden-apples scheme fail?

THE SEER OF DODONA

After the oracle at Delphi, the next most respected oracle in the world was the one who dwelled at the temple at Dodona. So respected was this oracle that the *Argo,* the ship that Jason and the Argonauts sailed in, was said to have prophetic powers of its own, simply because it was partially made from timber from this temple.

So when Aetolus, a Greek hero and son of Endymion, arrived there, entering the temple and striding manfully but unsteadily forward in full regalia (briefly tripping over some rubble from the restoration work in progress), the oracle regarded him with a wary but amused eye rather than a look of awe and respect.

"Now listen here," he began. "I have consulted many oracles across the land to learn my future. All of them have foreseen an imminent death for me but could not say how or why. I thought them all charlatans, no doubt in the pay of my enemies, and I put each of them to the sword! None of them saw that coming, I should say. So I have come here to seek the advice of the supposed 'great' oracle of Dodona. So tell me, woman: Am I to walk out of here to my doom?"

The oracle thought carefully, noting the sword in his hand.

*"Nothing bad will happen to you if you leave this
place," she said with quiet authority.*

Aetolus watched her for any signs of insincerity, then, apparently satisfied,
spun around and began clanking his way toward the exit.

The seer of Dodona's prophecy was true. But so were all the other prophecies
he had heard before.

 Question: How can all the oracles' prophecies be true?

A Pair of Kings

Before his imprisonment, King Tantalus was already a despicable individual, and his only match in nastiness was his friend Pandareus (who would later be turned to stone while helping Tantalus steal a mechanical dog, obviously).

One evening, Tantalus and Pandareus were dining on venison (once they had both ensured that they hadn't tried to poison each other).

"This is a bit stringy, cousin," Pandareus said acidly.
"Ah, you should taste the deer of the forest at the
time of the harvest season – that's when they
are fattest and juiciest," said Tantalus.
"Would that I could, but I have to be at my
own court at that time," said Pandareus.
"Well then, I will have a messenger bring you some
of the meat to enjoy there," declared Tantalus.
"It would have to be a very swift messenger. My kingdom is at
least five days from yours on foot, and inaccessible on horseback..."
Tantalus waved a dismissive hand. "I have the
fleetest messenger in the land! Oh, except that if
I send him, he may not return. He's recently been
rather grumpy about his constant punishments."

Suddenly Pandareus had an idea. "I have a poison that has no effect for six days, and then, when the sun rises on the seventh, it kills you on the spot! If I gifted you a bottle of that, and the antidote, you could give it to your messenger! Then he would have time to bring the venison to me and return to you to receive the antidote!"

"It is an excellent idea. But there's no need to provide me with the poison. I have exactly the same thing," said Tantalus.

And so, at the time of the harvest, the messenger was given the venison, poisoned, and sent on his way.

But the mountainous terrain and the weight of the venison meant that the messenger arrived at the court on the fourth day! He knew it would take him more than two days to return, even without the venison. And Pandareus knew that if the messenger did not return, Tantalus would assume foul play and declare war on his territory!

 Question: How can Pandareus ensure the messenger returns to Tantalus?

Making Sacrifices

The actors of the auditorium of Dionysus in Athens were preparing for the first performance of a new play by Cratinus, who at 97 was certainly the longest-lived playwright of his age, if not the best.

The *exarchon,* or leader of the group, announced that they would perform a sacrifice to Dionysus, the patron god of their auditorium and, indeed, of the cult that owned and maintained it.

"We will kill this goat in his name," the actor began.

"Only Dionysus?" said Cratinus loudly. "Why not Zeus? My play is a story of a family destroyed by a rude guest. Should we not pay tribute to he who is the lord of hospitality with a sacrifice of a bull?"

The actors turned in surprise at this sudden interruption, angered by the disrespect shown their patron god.

"Perhaps..." said the exarchon. "But..."

"And should we not make a sacrifice to Apollo? He is the lord of the arts, not to mention the sunlight that permits us to perform this play here today," continued Cratinus. "Should we not kill a swan for him?"

"We could..." said the exarchon.

The other actors muttered among themselves with agitation.

"And my play has a sea battle, so we must sacrifice a horse for

Poseidon! And sacrifice a second bull to Athena, as my play
has much wisdom within. And why not a sacrifice to Artemis,
to apologize for all the animals we are sacrificing?"
"Listen..." said the exarchon through gritted
teeth. "There can be only one sacrifice."
"But you are bound to disrespect at least one other god!"
shouted Cratinus. "They are petty and vengeful, and not
as civilized as you and me. Well, me at least."

 Question: What is the single sacrifice that the exarchon decided to make that would appease all the gods?

VRYKOLAKAS

Belief in the Vrykolakas was first recorded in the 17th century, but new manuscripts show its existence much longer before then. It has elements in common with werewolves and revenants in that it eats flesh and is known for being somewhat feral. But it is the vampire legend it most closely resembles.

One interesting parallel is with that of visiting houses. Some legends say that vampires cannot enter a house unless invited – an interesting connection with *xenia*. Vrykolakas, by comparison, were known to go around knocking on the front door of people's houses, and if the occupant answered after a single knock, they, too, would become a Vrykolakas.

A woman lived in a house next door to a very rowdy family that was often having large parties or arguing with each other. As the walls were thinly constructed, she felt like they were in the room with her!

One day she passed their house to find them dressed for a funeral. But no-one was chanting or wailing laments, and there was no visible body. Instead, they all looked pale and frightened. When she asked where the body was, they said with dread that he had blasphemed against the gods before slipping off a cliff, and therefore the body could not be recovered.

That night the woman was woken by a strange, cold feeling, and she was convinced that the dead man had risen as a Vrykolakas. As if in response to her thoughts, she heard a single sharp knock! She remained in bed, but mere moments later came another sharp knock on her front door, and she chided herself for being foolish, reasoning that it was probably her daughter returning from the temple. Sadly, she was wrong, and she answered the door and became a Vrykolakas within moments!

 Question: Why did the woman become a Vrykolakas when there were two knocks, not one?

PLUTO DWARFS HADES

The nature of the Underworld is so strange that time and space seem to decay and curdle in its presence, especially around the rivers.

So it came to be that Hades, on a walk by the Styx surveying his kingdom, slipped and fell in, and when he emerged, he was greeted by a hulking man twice his size, grinning with gold-plated teeth.

"Welcome to my kingdom," he leered.
"It's my kingdom..." rumbled Hades.
"No longer, sadly. I am Pluto – the improved model, shall we say?"
Pluto explained how, while Hades was feared and sometimes detested by the Greeks, his Roman version was treated with more respect due to the riches in his underground kingdom.
"Gold, jewels... You never took advantage of them," said Pluto smugly. "But I'm sure I can find you a position here. Maybe Charon would like to retire. How are you at sculling?"
Hades spat with contempt. "You are but a pale

shadow of me! I will reclaim my kingdom!"

"Yes, I remember you being pig-headed," said Pluto,
amused. "Very well, let's have a wager."

Pluto gestured and 10 gold coins appeared between his fingers,
numbered 1 to 10. He produced a velvet sack, which he emptied
of hundreds of gleaming jewels, and put the coins inside.

"Take three coins," he said, shaking the bag at Hades,
who did so, hiding them from Pluto.

"Now I'll take three for myself, and that leaves four in the bag,"
Pluto said, doing so. He put the bag on the ground.

"Listen, junior. If you can tell me which coins I have in my
hand, you can share this kingdom. But if not, your head can
be a chew toy for Cerberus. Yes, he's still around."

Hades peered at his coins. They were marked 3, 4 and 10.

As Pluto grinned, Hades tried to use his powers to see his coins, or at least foresee the result, but Pluto's powers of wealth were blocking him. All he could sense was that the coins in Pluto's hand, added together, had more value than the coins in the bag. Also, one or both of the values of the bag and Pluto's hand contained the number 4.

 Question: Which coins does Pluto have in his hand?

On the Fiddle

Hello! It's me! Nero! The mad emperor! The one who fiddled while Rome burned! Or did I burn while Rome fiddled?

I know what you're thinking. What's he doing in a book of myths? Wasn't he a real, devastatingly handsome Roman emperor? Well, I'm not *that* Nero – the boring, accurate one. I'm the myth! The metaphor! And you know how you can tell? Because I'm playing a fiddle! A violin! An instrument that did not exist in ancient Rome! So what did I actually play? Maybe it was a *cithara* – it's a bit like a lyre and a bit like a guitar. Or maybe I played a drum, or a flute. Or maybe I didn't play anything at all – I was just performing in a play!

Hit it, fellas! "Rome's Burning," in the key of G major! See, that's how you know I'm not the boring "real" Nero! Greek music didn't use the same chord structure as you do now! It's all quarter tones and Dorian modes. The songs were hymns and dithyrambs! Nothing you could really bop to.

Some say I didn't fiddle, or play music, or act when Rome burned! It was a story my enemies made up to discredit me. And what a story! I was accused of so many awful crimes – but it's the fiddle thing that really sticks in their head! Is it a sign of insanity? A metaphor for hubris or for the uncaring elite? An indicator of pure, unfiltered evil villainy? Perhaps we'll never know! They've debated for centuries what the key to it is! And now you know.

 Question: What is the key to Nero's fiddling while Rome burns?

192

193

THE CURSE OF NEPTUNE

The message that echoes across almost all the myths is simple: You cannot fight fate. Oracles would foresee people's deaths and great tragedies, and they could never avoid them. But despite this, they would always fight, or try to find a way around them.

Such was the case when Prince Charisius consulted the oracle at Delphi and was told, "Beware the curse...of Poseidon!"

"What curse? Am I cursed? Is Poseidon angry
at me?" he spluttered with confusion.
"I can say no more," the oracle said.
"What have I done? I've always respected Poseidon! Was
it that dolphin I slapped? If so, tell him I'm sorry!"
"I can say no more," the oracle again replied.
"How can I fix this? A sacrifice? What about a statue?"
"I can..."
"Say no more, yes, I know!"

194

Charisius marched off and ordered a *hecatomb* of cattle to be sacrificed to Poseidon and a big statue of Poseidon to be built, preferably with a lot of beautiful dolphins. But when he returned to Delphi, they simply repeated what they had said before: "Beware the curse of Poseidon!"

So he moved his palace away from the coast as far inland as possible, into a dry, barren area. No fountains, no running water near or into his palace. And then he eschewed drinking water, only drinking wine or other liquids. But even those frightened him, and he began to eschew those, too.

But it was to no avail. While he was not attacked or killed, and no disease or accident befell him, Charisius died soon after.

 Question: How did the curse of Poseidon kill Charisius?

ZEUS VS JUPITER

Zeus, the capricious, all-powerful, dreaded father of the Greek gods, feared few. Whether it was bravery, arrogance or ignorance, he was not scared of the chthonic deities like the Fates and the Furies, or the Titans that came before him, or even his own father, Cronus, whom he tricked into fetching up the other Olympian gods from his stomach after he had swallowed them.

He didn't fear Porphyrion the giant, and when the other gods became animals to flee from Typhon, he alone stood against them with his mighty thunderbolt.

So when one day he found himself face to face with Jupiter, his own Roman counterpart, he could not help but marvel at how scared he felt.

"Lightning may never strike in the same place twice," intoned Jupiter, his voice humming with energy. "But you are not lightning. You are the mere thunder that anticipated my arrival."
"No, we are the same," said Zeus carefully. "Two forks of the same strike. We need not battle."
"We are not the same," said Jupiter with menace. "I am you; it is true. And we both bear great power. But unlike you, I do not just submit to fate. I determine it. I control it. I AM FATE. And I cannot be defeated."
Zeus did not like this. "That is impossible," he said.
"Any game, any challenge you engage me in, I can only win," said Jupiter smugly.
"That is not true," said Zeus.

 Question: What challenge could Zeus set for Jupiter that Jupiter could not win?

1. Become Zeus
2. Feel fear
3. Lose

4. Fight Typhon
5. Trick Cronus

Zeusical Chairs

The 12 primary gods of Olympus were summoned to the throne room to discuss a vital matter: the Trojan War! The throne room had 12 thrones, each assigned to a particular occupant, with Zeus in the central throne (number 6) and Dionysus, the youngest god, in the 12th.

But Zeus looked addled, confused, unable to tell which was his throne. The other gods did not want to anger him or imply that he had been overpowered, so they didn't say anything.

"I think he has been enchanted by Eris, the goddess
of Chaos!" said Poseidon under his breath.
"Look, let's just wait for him to sit down," said Athena. "If he
sits in his throne, good. If he chooses one of ours, we'll all just
sit down one at a time in our proper thrones – except for the
displaced god, who can just choose another at random."
"But what if the displaced god sits in my throne?" asked Poseidon.
"Then you just choose at random too! It doesn't matter."

It does matter, thought Dionysus. He liked his throne; it was very comfortable and had its own grapevine. Now he had no idea what his chances were of getting to sit in it.

 Question: What is the percentage chance of Dionysus getting to sit in his own throne?

NEPTUNE VS POSEIDON

At the depths of the ocean is a darkness so total that the creatures there are born and die without ever seeing the sun. The wheel of time that the sun and moon mark across the sky holds no sway in the abyss, so it was down there that Neptune, Roman god of the sea, found his former incarnation, Poseidon, rising toward him with a furious expression.

"I have seen my brothers Hades and Zeus forced into conflict with their twisted reflections! So I have decided that I will strike the first blow personally..." Poseidon shouted.
"I have no quarrel with you," said Neptune. "Pluto and Jupiter think there can be only one. But you and I understand the ebb and flow of the tide, the ever-changing currents of the sea."
"I'm not interested in sharing anything," said Poseidon. "You are naught but a lesser version of myself. I am the god of the noble horse and you have abandoned that charge."
"But I inherited all the fresh waters of the world: the rivers, the lakes... You only rule the sea," said Neptune, wielding his trident warily.

"*The seas occupy seven-tenths of the earth's surface! The rivers and lakes are literally a mere drop in the ocean,*" *said Poseidon, getting ready to attack. "Well then, let us have a fight. Ten of my best river-boatmen, with no provisions and two horses, will sail three days along the Acheron River toward where it flows into the Ionian Sea. At the same time, 100 of your best sailors, with no provisions, will sail three days across the Ionian Sea to where the Acheron River joins it. When our two forces meet, they will fight, and the winner has dominion over seawater, freshwater and horses. Agreed?*"

Confident in his success, Poseidon agreed. He knew any of his sailors was a match for any of Neptune's boatmen, and he would have 10 times as many.

 Question: Why is Poseidon fated to lose this battle?

The Tale of Prometheus

"Tell me your story, Prometheus," said the eagle as it moved toward the man chained to the rock. "You know it, bird," said Prometheus with effort. "I stole fire from the gods. And this is my punishment: to be imprisoned here, and for you to eat my liver every day. A fitting penance for the most famous thief in history." "How?" the eagle asked curiously. "Am I stealing the liver from you? I don't understand. Did you commit any other crimes?" "It depends on what you call a crime. Some think me a mortal, but I was the one who created humanity from clay! I created Pandora, the first woman! That is why I stole the fire for them." "I see," said the eagle. "Strange. I

had heard that it was actually Hephaestus who made humanity from clay."
Prometheus shook his head.

"No. It was I. And it was I who taught humanity
about art, and mathematics, and philosophy."

"Hmm, was it not the muses and Athena who taught
mortals about the arts and sciences?" asked the eagle.

"Them? They came after me! I am a Titan, one of the gods that came
before the Olympian whelps that put me here. In fact, the Olympians
themselves would not exist without me! When the Titanomachy happened,
and my side fought against theirs, I was the one who aided them in
overthrowing Cronus and the others! Were these crimes? Perhaps to
the Olympians, who resent humanity and hate my kind, they are."
The eagle ruffled its feathers thoughtfully.

"It was my understanding that you are not one of the original
Titans, but a mere descendent who bears the same name," said the
eagle. "And the Titans were overthrown by the Olympians' cunning,
not your own. You are indeed history's most famous thief. But
other than fire, I can think of only one thing you have stolen."

 Question: What is the one thing, besides fire, that the eagle thinks Prometheus has stolen?

Psyche and Cupid
Part I: Mr. Bug Goes to Lunch

A mortal woman named Psyche was renowned as a great beauty; and Venus, the original wicked queen, was so jealous she sent her son Cupid to use his arrows and make Psyche fall in love with the most hideous creature possible. In the original myths he was not a sweet little angel but a sometimes dangerous god of mischief.

Cupid accidentally nicked himself with one of his love darts and fell in love with Psyche. A series of misunderstandings led to their brief union, which angered Venus further, and eventually a distraught Psyche ended up in the cruel hands of Cupid's vengeful mother.

Imprisoning her in a house, Venus feared angering Jupiter if she was not a good host. But she had to get rid of her somehow. So she put the poor, starving Psyche in a room filled with a mass of lentils, beans, barley and wheat.

"Sort these into individual piles, girl!" Venus spat. "You may eat one of each, but no more! I will return in two hours!"

She slammed the door and Psyche wept at her hopeless task. But then she saw a tiny ant nearby, with hundreds of his brothers behind him.

"Sorting beans, huh?" he said. "We could do that in two hours, no problem. Probably with one minute to spare. But it'll cost ya, and I don't think you've got anything we want. So it looks like your phoenix is cooked."

Psyche thought. "If you sort the piles for me... you may then eat as much as you wish."

"OK, deal," said the ant greedily. This foolish girl doesn't know how quickly we can eat, he thought. The second we're done, we'll chow down on the whole pile in 30 seconds and there'll be nothing left to show Venus. But that's her problem."

However, when Venus arrived, there were neat piles of each type of food, and only one missing seed or kernel from each. Psyche's intuition had paid off.

 Question: Why were the piles of food still almost all there when Venus arrived?

Part II: Feeling Sheepish

Venus was enraged by Psyche's success and sought another task to endanger her.

"I need to knit myself a shawl, child," Venus said imperiously.
"There are some sheep who graze on the other side of the river near here. Go fetch me some of their wool. You cannot miss them. They are golden sheep."

Sure that this was some kind of trick, Psyche set out toward the river. She had heard tell of Helios' flock of golden sheep (which went nicely with his cattle) grazing nearby. She knew that, although they might seem docile, they were in fact vicious killers.

She was wrong, but only about the first part. They didn't seem docile at all, and as she approached the river she saw them on the other side, with eyes of fury and surprisingly sharp teeth and horns, butting up against each other and at anything that came near them in a frenzy! She could possibly sneak near them, but she was sure if she tried to get any wool from them at all she would be assaulted instantly!

At this point she despaired. Either the sheep would get her, or Venus would punish her harshly for her failure. As she made her way down to the water, her ragged clothes became tangled in the sharp briars that grew profusely on both banks of the river, and she considered simply throwing herself into the stream.

"Do not despair!" whispered a voice, and Psyche realized it
was one of the reeds by the river singing musically to her.
"But I am caught in the currents of the lives of the gods, destined
to be dashed against the rocks of fate," she replied.
"No, you are merely entangled with them. And the
nimblest fingers can extract the thread of fate."

Psyche nodded and stood up. She knew what she needed to do.

 Question: How can Psyche obtain the golden wool without being killed by the sheep?

Part III: Eagle vs Dragons

Once again, Venus was enraged by Psyche's success. And she knew that her son was seeking Psyche too, so she had to act fast.

"Child, I am, um...thirsty. Get me some of the black water that flows from the source of the Styx," she shouted, giving Psyche a crystal vessel and pushing her out the door.

Psyche made her way up the steep mountainside. As she walked, everything around her was ashen, bereft of all life...except dragons! They slithered around the area watching with hungry eyes. She knew their curiosity would soon turn to violence, and fell into despair.

Jupiter, sensing this, sent an eagle.

208

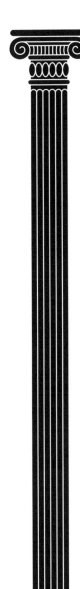

It flew swiftly and landed near Psyche. A few dragons were already approaching.

"Out of the way, lizards," said the eagle. "I have to get
back to Prometheus, so you had better make room for me
to escort Psyche to the source of the Styx right now."
"An eagle?" said one with a contemptuous
snarl. "Sent by Jupiter, I suppose."
"You are correct," said the eagle.
"And he has endowed you with all sorts of incredible
powers?" asked the dragon pointedly.
"No more incredible than I already had. I can fly and see
quite far. I can peck things. My claws can pick up mice."
"My claws could slice a Manticore in two," said
the dragon, unsheathing an enormous talon.
"Or make a shish kebab of a tiny bird."
The other dragons all laughed with lizard-like hisses,
demonstrating their own teeth and talons.
"I'm not afraid of you," said the eagle.
"Why not? We are dozens of enormous dragons,
almost as powerful as a god, and you are a tiny,
normal eagle. We can easily defeat you."
"I do not fear defeat," said the eagle.
"I think what he is hinting at," said Psyche, suddenly looking up,
"is that you need to consider the consequences of your actions."

 Question: Why do the dragons allow the eagle to escort Psyche to the source and then leave?

209

PART IV: GOING TO THE DOGS

Venus couldn't believe that Psyche had somehow survived the trip, especially since Psyche omitted the eagle's aid. For this reason, she decided on one final deadly task.

"Take this pyxis *and get some more beauty for me, will you,"*
Venus said casually, handing Psyche a small box.
"Beauty? From where?"
"Why, you must go down into the Underworld and obtain it
from Proserpina. She has plenty to spare," said Venus nastily.

Proserpina was the Roman name for Penelope, making her the wife of Pluto, the king of the Underworld.

But Psyche could not refuse. She left with the box. But rather than descend into the Underworld, she climbed a huge tower, planning to throw herself off the top.

But the tower itself spoke to her! It told her where to find an entrance to the Underworld, and told her to check a room on its ground floor. In a cupboard there she found two coins for her eyes, and five more *pyxides*.

After she entered the Underworld and had made her way past various deceptions, she saw Cerberus, the three-headed guard dog, blocking her way!

She remembered what the tower had told her. In the five pyxides it had given her were honey-barley cakes to be fed to Cerberus. The tower had instructed her that each head of Cerberus had to eat the same amount of cakes: one *hēmina!* Knowing that there were six *kyathoi* in one hēmina, and 10 *Kochliara* in a kyathoi, she opened the boxes to inspect their contents:

- Pyxis 1 was a hēmina-sized box, three-fifths full.
- Pyxis 2 was another hēmina box, completely full.
- Pyxis 3 was a two-hēmina box, but was only a third full.
- Pyxis 4 was smaller, a two-kyathoi box, totally full.
- Pyxis 5 was a six-kyathoi box, two-fifths full.

 Question: Which boxes should be given to which heads to make sure they all get the same?

Part V: Ambrosia Cocktail

And so, Psyche reached Proserpina. And the queen of the Underworld was amused, and relished an opportunity to get one up on her rival, Venus. So she told Psyche that she had put some of her beauty inside the small *pyxis* that Cupid's mother had given Psyche, then sent Psyche back up to the overground.

Some retellings of the story say that Psyche became too curious about what was inside the box and opened it in the hope of making herself more beautiful. But inside was actually a spell of infernal sleep that Proserpina hoped to inflict on Venus, and Psyche was cursed by it until Cupid found and rescued her.

But that doesn't fit our resourceful heroine; so let's imagine instead that Psyche made it to the surface, and that Venus was waiting there malevolently after hearing of her surprising success. Psyche convinced her that there was beauty in the pyxis, so Venus snatched the box from her hands and shoved her face right into it, then collapsed immediately into a deep slumber.

Psyche found Cupid, and the two went to Olympus to entreat the gods. And Jupiter, looking kindly on their union (after getting Cupid to promise that he'd receive notice of any attractive women the young god spotted), declared that Venus would leave them alone and Psyche would be made immortal, provided she could successfully mix the ambrosian elixir.

"It has four ingredients, my dear," Jupiter said. "And if you use them in the wrong quantities, you will be cursed or transformed into a monster, or, worst of all, be forced to listen to one of Neptune's fishing stories."
"Hey!" said Neptune.
"Listen well, child: 16 ligula of the vessel must not contain ambrosia; 15 ligula must not have any nectar; 13 ligula must be free of Styx water; and 19 ligula of it will not have any ichor. Good luck."
Psyche nodded.

 Question: In what quantities must Psyche use each of these ingredients?

END OF THE CENTURY

In modern language, a century is 100 years. But the other idea of a century, or *centuria* – that of 100 military units – has not always been set in stone. From about 100 BC to roughly the end of the Roman empire, a century meant 80 men, with a centurion in charge of them.

The reasons for this are disputed. Some say it was simply a matter of not having enough troops to have 100 men in each group. Others say it would be a group of 80 career soldiers and 20 support troops, possibly slaves, who therefore were not considered to be worth counting. It's worth considering that, as the empire began to struggle, many of these groups wouldn't even have 80 men, due to death or desertion, and the recorded numbers were simply manipulated to make things seem better than they were.

For this reason, any mathematics using a "century" as a unit of measurement might differ wildly, depending on when you were calculating it. However:

$$100 \times a = b$$
$$80 \times a = c$$

Looking at these two equations, there is a value for *a* that would mean *b* and *c* have the same result.

 Question: What value should *a* be?

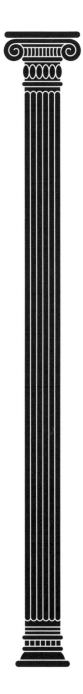

215

Sphinx of the Riddle

Oedipus had had quite a day. The oracle at Delphi had told him in quite clear terms that he would kill his father and marry his mother. Seeking to avoid this fate, he had left the land of his parents, King Polybus and Queen Merope, and departed for the city of Thebes to seek his fortune.

On the way, Oedipus ended up in a quarrel with a wanderer on the road that ended in the wanderer's death! Then, when he arrived at Thebes, Oedipus found out that their king had recently been murdered by an unknown assailant! Bad luck for him – and for the city, too – as a sphinx had taken the opportunity to take over the city. Sphinxes were demonic entities that craved destruction and brought bad tidings wherever they went. An enormous creature with a woman's head, lion's body and eagle wings, the sphinx roamed the city attacking everything and refusing to leave unless someone could answer her riddle. (Some think the sphinx is an Egyptian myth, but statues found in Egypt were of an older, unnamed creature, and were nicknamed sphinxes by ancient Greek tourists.)

Oedipus confronted the sphinx in a wrecked marketplace, and there was something about him that made her pause.

"Oedipus," she purred. "Oh boy, are you in for a surprise. But not from me."

"Enough stalling, demon! Tell me the riddle!" Oedipus declared.
"Understand, Oedipus: I see all of time. I can see my own birth and
my own demise. I see your terrible fate and how it plays out. But I
also see our futures. Mine as a misnamed statue in a country I have
never visited. Yours as a metaphor for serious psychological issues."
"Enough of your nonsense, creature! The riddle!"
The sphinx smiled.
"I see everything. The births and deaths of every human, every creature. I see
seeds grow into trees, frogspawn turn into frogs, meadows become deserts. I
even see people reading this story, written in a book far in the future, expecting
a particular riddle, one with an answer that almost everyone already knows."
The sphinx turns to look at you.
"But I have a new riddle for you – very similar to the original. And
if you cannot solve it, then the fall of Thebes is on your hands."

 **Question: What has two legs in the morning, three legs
in the afternoon and four legs in the evening?**

HANNIBAL CROSSES THE ALPS

Hannibal, the Carthaginian general who led the effort against the Roman empire in the second Punic wars, is primarily known for the incredible military achievement of getting his troops up and down the Alps to allow them to attack Rome while bypassing many Roman ground troops and without having to sail through Roman-dominated seas – all while using elephants, which, while not uncommon as a military resource for Carthaginians, could have been bypassed in this circumstance.

What is sometimes not referenced is that this wasn't just an exhausting hiking expedition. It also contained a series of military battles and skirmishes that had to be carefully negotiated.

By the time Hannibal came to the Alps, he had already lost about 10,000 troops, some by death and some by being dismissed or sent elsewhere. He began his ascent with 50,000 men in all fighting disciplines.

They anticipated an ambush by a tribe of Barbarians and were able to provoke them into springing their own trap; but by the time they had succeeded in battle, his troops were reduced by 16%.

Luckily a friendly tribe, the Centrones, bolstered them with supplies and relief troops, and his troop number then increased by 10%.

But subsequently – due to roads blocked by avalanches needing labour to clear them and another, more successful ambush by another tribe – Hannibal's troops were ultimately reduced by 10% before he came to the place where he could descend to Rome.

 Question: How many troops did Hannibal have when he began his descent to Rome?

Unicorns!

The unicorn is now such a ubiquitous fantasy creature that it is easy to forget its Greek origins. While it's true that the idea of a single-horned horse occurs in pre-Greek manuscripts and art, it was through their writings that the idea really took shape, before being adopted with enthusiasm during the Middle Ages. One of the earliest writings on the subject was by Ctesias, a historian and physician who believed that unicorns lived in India – although he also said they were black and red, apart from the usual white-haired variety.

Yet unicorns do not occur anywhere in Greek mythology. Considering the number of creatures they did discuss, of which this book barely scratches the surface, there are no unicorns in any of the stories of gods or heroes. There are other horse creatures, like Centaurs and the famous Pegasus, but no unicorns. There are creatures even more incredible, like Charybdis, an enormous underwater creature whose mouth formed a giant whirlpool; and Laelaps, a legendary dog that could not fail to catch whatever it was hunting. But those who wrote Greek myths would not include the unicorn.

 Question: Why wasn't the unicorn present in ancient Greek mythology?

PHYLLIS-OPHICAL

One of the greatest, most enduring mysteries in classical mythology is that of Phyllis and Demophon.

Demophon was the king of Athens and one of Theseus' sons. Phyllis, his wife, was said to be the daughter of a king, but which one differs in the retelling, with most thinking it was King Sithon of the Odomanti. Some doubt that this was true, and think that she had some other connection to royalty.

Nonetheless, she lived in Thrace, and when Demophon stopped there on his return from the Trojan war they quickly fell in love and married. She begged him to remain there with her, saying that it was rare for her to receive a gift like his love, and she wanted to hold onto it. But he was duty bound to return home. He promised her that he would return, and she gave him a casket, making him promise to open it only if he had given up hope of returning to her.

Many retellings of the story say that the box contained a sacrament of Rhea, the Titaness earth goddess, who was a child of Gaia. They say that when she decided that Demophon would never return, she took her own life and became an almond (or hazelnut tree).

Some retellings say that Demophon, too curious, opened the box and was so shocked by what he saw that he fell off his horse and, fatally, onto his own sword!

But they do not say what was inside the box.

But the new evidence that we have access to has allowed us to finally understand the truth of Phyllis and her casket – why it inspired such curiosity, and why she said he should open it only when he was without hope. Maybe it helps to think that it may not have been a casket, but instead a *pyxis,* or jar.

 Question: Who was Phyllis, and what was in the casket?

Troy, Troy Again

The Trojan war supposedly began when Eris, the goddess of chaos, was not invited to a wedding party attended by many of the other gods, so she threw a magical golden apple marked "for the fairest" into the room. Hera, Aphrodite and Athena all thought the apple should be theirs. They chose a young shepherd to decide this, not realizing he was Paris, a Trojan prince. Ultimately, he accepted Aphrodite's offer: the love of any woman in the world.

Paris chose Helen of Troy, the most beautiful woman that had ever lived. So Aphrodite worked her magic and Helen left her husband, the Greek King Menelaus, for Paris. Menelaus then declared war on Troy to get his wife back.

Many battles and events followed, with the gods' intervention and changing sides leading to shock developments like the death of Achilles and, eventually, the siege of Troy. And by the time the Greek army built the horse and then sailed away, leaving it as a "gift," the weary, half-starved Trojans may not have thought it so strange considering the deaths that had already occurred on both sides. Peace may have seemed worth the risk.

Nonetheless, while the Trojans slept, the 40 warriors crept out of the horse and sacked the city, killing sleeping citizens and opening the gate for the now returned Greek army to flood inside. Helen's attitude to this is reported differently; some say she tried to see if there were men inside by imitating the voices of their loved ones outside, to no avail. Others say she knew about the trick and aided it by throwing a distracting festival.

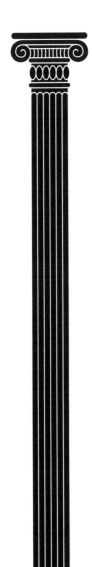
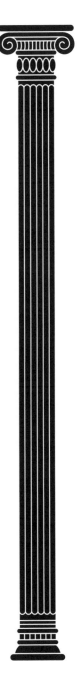

It took 40 people to overthrow the city. But it could be said that if the Trojans had done the same and given a wooden horse to the Greeks during the siege, it would have needed only one person inside to end the war.

 Question: How could one person inside the wooden horse end the war?

YOU'LL NEVER OUTFOX THE FOX

Amphitryon had a challenging problem. His wife, Alcmene, had refused to marry him until he defeated the Taphians, who had killed all but one of her brothers. And he couldn't defeat them unless he had the help of Creon. And Creon would not help him unless he got rid of the Teumessian fox!

"It's a wily creature that Dionysus has set on the Theban countryside,"
Creon said as they crouched behind a bush. "It chases all who see it
and tries to eat them – especially children!"
"Well then, we'll catch it," said Amphitryon, getting out
one of his better nets.
"That's the thing: It's uncatchable. That's its power,
besides being large and clever. It is literally its
destiny to never be caught," said Creon bitterly.
"We'll see about that!" said Amphitryon,
rubbing his hands together.

So he tried everything. Nets, pit traps, spears, arrows, teams of men, disguises, pushing giant boulders, and even painting a fake tunnel on a wall. But to no avail. The fox was always one step ahead, and seemed merely amused by the attempts to catch the uncatchable!

In the end, Amphitryon had only one idea left. He would use a creature mentioned in one of the previous puzzles in this book. Even this course of action might not lead to the fox being caught, but he reasoned that, at the very least, it would bring events to a conclusion.

 Question: Which creature did Amphitryon get to set on the uncatchable Teumessian fox?

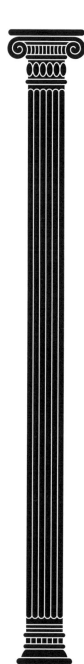
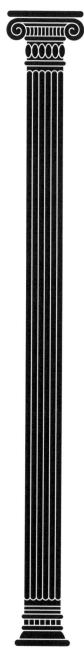

CONSTELLATION PRIZE

Many of the classical myths in this book were not only stories to explain things about nature or philosophy, or consider the nature of fate, or simply entertain people. They also served a more scientific purpose, as the gods, heroes, and monsters within were often also constellations, groupings of stars that allowed them to know their position, and sometimes navigate on land or at sea.

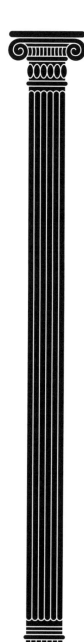

 Question: Here are 10 different constellations. Which myth does each represent? The final one is a more modern constellation, but perhaps its name will give a clue as to which ancient constellation it was once connected with.

- Gemini: Mirrored siblings, faithfully aiding a quest for a magical object.
- Canis major and minor: Hunter and prey, eternally circling.
- Sagitta: A weapon that flies and hopefully finds its mark – whether bird, beast or one-eyed monster.
- Draco: A scaled monstrosity with fiery breath.
- Leo: An indestructible beast with a single vulnerability.
- Aquila: A bird assigned to both punishment and rescue by its master.
- Centaurus: Neither man nor beast, but both.
- Auriga: A pilot of a two-wheeled vehicle used in races and sometimes transport.
- Lyra: An instrument privileged to play the greatest music.
- Carina: The lowest part of a famous seagoing vessel.

SOLUTIONS

SOLUTIONS

PG. 8 TROJAN HORSE

The horse would be 9.6 feet wide, 24.8 feet tall, and 14.4 feet long. The horse is 20% smaller than the original plan because 40 is 20% less than 50. *Pous* is the equivalent of the modern "foot," because that's where the term originally came from!

PG.10 ESCAPING THE LABYRINTH

If he walks with his hand on the left wall and keeps it there moving forward, they will inevitably find the exit.

PG. 12 PERSEUS AND THE HESPERIDES

They are in the following order:
1) Donakis; 2) Mermesa;
3) Aiopis; 4) Nelisa; 5) Tara;
6) Calypso; 7) Antheia. Therefore, Calypso has the kibisis.

PG. 14 PANDORA'S JAR

Security–Threat. Harmony–Discord. Fairness–Injustice. Mercy–Cruelty. Peace–Conflict. Joy–Sadness. Health–Illness. Sanity–Madness. Knowledge–Ignorance. Hope–Despair. Freedom has no match; therefore, ironically, it is the thing that remained trapped.

PG. 16 DIP STYX

Achaeus: Hand or finger. Bienor: Ear or ears. Caucon: Hair. Demodice: Elbow (tennis elbow). Epicasta: Knee.

PG. 18 CIRCE'S CURSES

The drunkard became the fish, drinking only pure water. The hermit became the wolf, moving always with a pack. The idler became the magpie, constantly darting from place to place. The thief became the snail, unable to take any of the treasure. The pirate became the tortoise, doomed to dullness and slowness. And the murderer became the deer, vulnerable and hunted.

SOLUTIONS

PG. 20 HERCULES' FIRST LABOUR: THE NEMEAN LION

He used the dead lion's claw. The lions' skins could be penetrated by them, as shown by their ability to slash and kill each other. So he was able to stab it and then skin it with the claw.

PG. 22 THE SECOND LABOUR: THE LERNAEAN HYDRA

Five. It takes 30 seconds to sever the head, 30 seconds for two to grow in its place, and 29 to cauterize. When Iolaus arrives, the first head has been growing back for 15 seconds. He begins cauterizing, but after 15 seconds two new heads spring up, meaning the beast now has four, except Hercules then succeeds at severing the next head so it's back to three. Iolaus begins cauterizing this one while Hercules hacks at the next, and therefore he prevents any more growing, as he can always cauterize before any grow back. Once Hercules has severed the third original head, he can return to the two new ones and chop them off to be cauterized – therefore five.

PG. 24 THE THIRD LABOUR: THE CERYNEIAN HIND

The hind's speed is double that of a normal arrow, so 600km per hour. When the arrow is initially fired it begins at 300km an hour and accelerates by 1km a second every minute. 600km per hour is 10km per minute. 300km an hour is 5km per minute. 1km a second is 60km per minute. So when the arrow is fired, after the first minute the hind has travelled 10km and the arrow has travelled 5km, putting it 15km away from the hind (as it was already 10km away). The arrow now speeds up to 65km a minute! The hind now travels another 10km, but the arrow travels 65km and, as the hind was only 15km away, the arrow easily covers the 25km and hits the hind in the leg.

233

SOLUTIONS

PG. 25 THE FOURTH LABOUR: THE ERYMANTHIAN BOAR

The sun. At dawn the boar ran west, as the sun came up in the east, and as it changed position in the sky the boar ran in different directions, ending up running to the east as the sun went down in the west. Apollo drives the sun chariot, and the boar thought he was being hunted by him.

PG. 26 THE FIFTH LABOUR: AUGEAN STABLES

There were 3,000 cattle (Hercules was promised 10% of them, which was stated to be 300). They each produced 30kg of manure a day, which is 90,000kg a day in total. 30 years = 10,950 days, not counting leap years. 10,950 x 90,000 = 985,500,000kg!

PG. 28 THE SIXTH LABOUR: DEFEAT THE STYMPHALIAN BIRDS

He drained the mountain lake, then stood at the bottom. Like the hollow *pithos,* the bowl shape of the empty lake acted as a natural amplifier.

PG. 30 THE SEVENTH LABOUR: CAPTURE THE CRETAN BULL

It wandered to Marathon. Philippides famously ran from Marathon to Athens to deliver crucial information; and in 1893 the founders of the modern Olympic Games included a special race that spans 42.195km, the supposed distance of Philippides' run, creating the marathon as we understand it today.

PG. 32 THE EIGHTH LABOUR: THE MARES OF DIOMEDES

The trough horse must be Lampon, as it cannot see Hercules but is not asleep. That means the horse lying on the ground must be Xanthos, as it is the only other yellow one. Therefore, Podargos the swift is leaning on the tree, because the other horse can see Hercules, meaning it must be Deinos the terrible.

SOLUTIONS

PG. 34 THE NINTH LABOUR: THE BELT OF HIPPOLYTA

Seven left, and seven arrived. There were four sons of King Minos, and they killed a third of Hercules' men. Hercules killed half of them (two) and took the remaining people as a replacement. As there are only two left, that means there must have been six men originally (two is one-third of six); so six and Hercules arrived and left.

PG. 36 THE TENTH LABOUR: THE CATTLE OF GERYON

4, 2, 5, 8, 6, 9, 10, 7, 3, 1.

PG. 38 THE ELEVENTH LABOUR: THE GOLDEN APPLES OF THE HESPERIDES

b) That a huge monster is coming. On the misty isle, the lamps would look like huge glowing eyes, and the krotala made a loud, terrible sound.

a) Would not trick Atlas, as he has held the sky for a long time and knows it is tough. And c) would not work, because the Old Man of the Sea said that everyone knows of Eurystheus' hatred of Hercules.

PG. 40 THE TWELFTH LABOUR: CAPTURE CERBERUS

He should use none of the three doors, but the place where he entered, in Acherusia. The riddle has been spoken by Cerberus, who could therefore be lying about every aspect of it. The priest told Hercules to remember that tales serve the purpose of the teller, and it would serve Cerberus' purpose for Hercules to be imprisoned. Instead it is better for him to go back and exit the way he entered.

SOLUTIONS

PG. 42 THE FALL OF ICARUS

Clouds. On the first two days it was much cloudier; there had recently been a storm, as evidenced by the dimmer daylight, choppy seas and increased humidity. But as the days wore on, the light in the distance and the higher-flying birds showed it was passing, and on their flight day there was a bright blue sky with a sun unobstructed by any cloud cover, in an ideal position to melt his wings.

PG. 44 THE QUEST OF PERSEUS

c) 1-8-3. You achieve this by subtracting the number of letters in each suitor's name from the number of the tower their head is mounted on. 11-10 = 1; 15-7 = 8; 9-6 = 3.

PG. 46 PERSEUS PART II: FIFTY SHADES OF GRAEAE

Pemphredo, because she is the one who currently has the eye and she would therefore have to pass the eye to one of her sisters so that Perseus could steal it.

PG. 48 PERSEUS PART III: SNAKE GOOD HAIR OF YOURSELF

The first path. Perseus' aim is not to avoid seeing Medusa (he has the shield) but to avoid Medusa seeing him. The first path's many statues mean that he can hide behind them as he approaches before going in for the kill.

PG. 50 PERSEUS PART IV: GOING, GOING, GORGON

The fourth tunnel. Lakes don't have waves (still water), dripping slime, fire or subterranean rumbling, but often have wildlife, like birds.

PG. 52 PERSEUS PART V: GET A HORSE

The second one. The first horse has the wings of an ostrich, which is a flightless bird. The second has eagle wings.

SOLUTIONS

PG. 54 PERSEUS PART VI: PERSEUS VS CETUS

He needs to block the creature's blowhole, through which it is able to breathe even if its mouth and nose are sealed.

PG. 56 PERSEUS PART VII: THE FINAL CHAPTER

King Polydectes. Knowing that Perseus had the head, he had deliberately plunged his palace into darkness so that he could not gaze at it and be turned into stone. Unfortunately for him, Perseus already had practice moving around in complete darkness.

PG. 58 NARCISSUS

Because his image was flipped left to right; therefore his hair was parted differently, his hair clasp was on the other side of his head, and his bracer was on the wrong arm.

PG. 60 HYPNOS

The fourth day. On the first day he slept 6 hours (6 out of 8 in a 24-hour cycle). On the second, the double of 6 is 12. On the third day, $3 \times 6 = 18$. On the fourth day, 18 hours of wakefulness plus 6 hours of wakefulness makes 24. The fifth and sixth days also add up to 24.

PG. 61 SISYPHUS

The boulder has moss growing on it. As the adage says, a rolling stone gathers no moss.

PG. 62 PART I: XENIA AND THE WARRIOR PRINCE

Because Iobates was obligated by xenia to welcome Bellerophon as a guest before he asked him his business. Therefore, he couldn't read the tablet until Bellerophon was already his guest and covered by xenia. In fact, Iobates didn't read the tablet until nine days later!

SOLUTIONS

PG. 64 PART II: CAPTURING PEGASUS

The shady glen would be the best place to capture Pegasus. The river is too wide open, and the waterfall would be filled with creatures that could either attack him or alert the horse. But the glen was more enclosed, and the fermented fruit dropping into the water could make it mildly alcoholic, impairing Pegasus' abilities.

PG. 66 PART III: THE CHIMERA

A: Griffin; B: Harpy; C: Satyr; D: Echidna; E: Centaur; F: Pegasus

PG. 68 PART IV: EAT LEAD, CHIMERA!

The tablet that bore Iobates' message. It was made of lead, and therefore could be affixed to the end of his spear.

PG. 71 PART V: BOLDER ADVENTURES

They would both be hit at the same time. The weight of the boulders is immaterial; they would both drop at the same speed due to the momentum cancellation effect.

PG. 72 PART VI: THE STING

The ant. Spiders can't fly (and are arachnids), and houseflies, butterflies and hoverflies can't sting. There are, however, many species of ant that sting and fly.

PG. 74 DEMETER AND PERSEPHONE

The seeds were planted in 1798 BC, and then the plant grew a year later.

PG. 76 PIECES OF PELOPS

Four. The first time she stirs it, the order will become 3, 4, 1, 5, 2, 6, 7. The second time, it becomes 3, 1, 4, 2, 5, 6, 7. The third, it becomes 1, 3, 2, 4, 5, 6, 7. On the fourth stir, it finally becomes 1, 2, 3, 4, 5, 6, 7.

SOLUTIONS

PG. 78 THE TORMENT OF TANTALUS

c) Stand on his head. None of the others are possible. He can't leave the pool; shaking the tree in any way won't dislodge fruit; and jumping does not work. However, it is only when he is standing on his feet that the branches raise up. If he stood on his head he could, with effort, pick a piece of fruit with his feet.

PG. 79 A ZEUS CONNECTION

He is his own great-great-grandfather.

PG. 80 PART I: THE CREW

Perseus. He was Hercules' great-grandfather, as shown in a previous puzzle.

PG. 81 PART II: ARGO ROW

Because they all sat on the same side of the ship, which then went in circles.

PG. 82 PART III: CYZICUS' PARTY

Hercules. Hercules was a drover when he moved the cattle of Geryon, a musician when he used the rattle to scare the Stymphalian birds, a weightlifter when he took the weight of the sky from Atlas, a spelunker when he went into the Underworld to fight Cerberus, and a hydrological engineer when he diverted the rivers to wash out the Augean stables.

PG. 83 PART IV: JOURNEY INTO DARKNESS

Because they were the Doliones, the group the Argonauts had just left. In the darkness, by steering west, south, further west, double east and then north, they had come all the way around the coast, back to the beach where they had landed previously. The palace had been made dark to mourn their supposed death, so when they arrived they were mistaken for an invading army.

SOLUTIONS

PG. 84 PART V: POLLUX VS AMYCUS

Because when he was young, Amycus was dipped in the river Styx by his mother, just as Achilles would be many years later. Amycus' strange invulnerability suggested a magical source, and his familiarity with the Underworld and Charon suggested a connection with the Styx. When he said his mother had taken him by the arm and bathed him, Pollux remembered the story of Achilles and correctly guessed that his arm had not been dipped in all the way.

PG. 86 PART VI: PHINEAS AND HERBS

The flakes from his enchanted chiton. By sprinkling them in the food, he knows the Harpies can't attack or eat it.

PG. 88 PART VII: THE DOVE FROM ABOVE

They would need to be moving around 80km/h, a third faster than the dove. The dove's tail got caught, and that is a third of its length (10cm of 30cm). So if they went through at the same speed, it's likely that a third of their boat would be crushed behind them. If they travel a third faster, they should make it out in time.

PG. 90 PART VIII: DEATH IN THE WILD

A boar: short and hairy, with a beard and two tusks (curved spears), known for goring people in the thigh and attacking relentlessly. Hercules fought the Erymanthian Boar and Perseus fought Cetus, the half-boar, half-whale monster.

SOLUTIONS

PG. 91 PART IX: STYMPHALIAN RESURRECTION

By clashing their spears against their shields! This would create a loud rattling noise similar to the krotala, and scare the birds away.

PG. 92 PART X: YOKE THE BULLS

Because the bulls see in infrared – meaning only heat. That's why they attack fires but not cold objects. Pollux confused them because he was cooled by the lake, and the blanket will mask Jason's body heat.

PG. 94 PART XI: SHOULDN'T SOWING DRAGON'S TEETH GIVE YOU DRAGONS?

Into the middle. Although the hit is not guaranteed, the ricochet will make it seem as if the stone has come from the direction of the first group, whereas the other two hits will more obviously come from the direction of where Jason is hiding.

PG. 96 PART XII: HOW TO TAME HIS DRAGON

The fourth path. While the others all have visible dangers, the dragon's mouth is closed. Jason knows that 100 dragon's teeth were sown to create the warriors; therefore the dragon is probably now toothless, which is why it took it so long to eat the sheep.

PG. 98 PART XIII: CIRCE'S BACK

Surprisingly, yes. Even though it seems counterintuitive, Jason has more of a chance of getting the right potion by switching than by remaining with his original choice. When he makes his first choice there is a ⅓ chance of bottle 1 containing the right potion and ⅔ chance of it being the other two. However, when Circe demonstrates that bottle two has the goat potion, it means bottle three has a ⅔ chance of being correct. This is known as the Monty Hall problem and is a classic probability paradox.

SOLUTIONS

PG. 100 PART XIV: SIRENS' SONG

1-1-1-1-1. The numbers he plays are a factor of the original number. But the Sirens' tune is all prime numbers, which have only two factors: 1 and themselves. Therefore, Orpheus just has to play the same note over and over (which would explain why he's so bummed out).

PG. 102 PART XV: THE TALE OF TALOS

Talos is a machine, because if you observe the number of steps he takes, they represent odd numbers descending (9, 7, 5) alternating with even numbers rising (2, 4, 6), forming a mathematical pattern.

PG. 104 PELOPS' PROGRESS

Pelops had the inside track and, as the drunken gods forgot to stagger their start, and used the same starting line, he had a shorter journey and would easily complete 12 laps before they did.

PG. 105 TARQUIN'S HAT

The eagle may have mistaken his hat for prey (a wolf cub) and snatched it up to kill and eat; but then, as it flew on, it saw the statue of the she-wolf and, mistaking it for the cub's mother, placed it back where it had found it so as not to anger her.

PG. 106 THE COUNTERFEIT COIN

Bite it. The coin may weigh the same and look the same, but copper is harder than gold. So simply biting each of them should reveal the counterfeit. Newborn babies have no teeth.

PG. 108 A FLAMING TRICKY PUZZLE

1: Crow; 2: Man; 3: Stag; 4: Raven; 5: Phoenix

SOLUTIONS

PG. 109 WHERE'S SPARTACUS?
Cartacus. Neither Artacus or Eartacus can be Spartacus, as he must tell the truth and would not say that someone else is him. Bartacus can't be Spartacus, as no-one else can tell the truth, so he couldn't say that. Dartacus can't be Spartacus, because if Cartacus is lying, that means both Eartacus and Bartacus are telling the truth, which is impossible. And Felix can't be Spartacus, because if everyone else is lying, then that means there are too many truth-tellers. Only Cartacus telling the truth and everyone else lying is logically possible.

PG. 110 THE FIRST LABOUR: THE CLUB OF PERIPHETES
He didn't hit the stick, but instead hit Periphetes over the head with the club. He hit him two times when he wasn't expecting it and left with the club as his trophy.

PG. 112 THE SECOND LABOUR: SINIS THE TREE-SPLITTER

Theseus simply released the first tree, and Sinis was catapulted up and forward, shattering his body on the cliff face!

PG. 113 THE THIRD LABOUR: THE CROMMYONIAN SOW
Because he suspects it is in fact the wise woman transformed. She is a were-pig, destined to turn into the sow at night, as evidenced by the acorns and mud bath she keeps in her house. The cage is designed to keep her in during her transformation, which is why there had been fewer attacks recently; but she had apparently broken out of it and trashed her house. The gods may help her – if it wasn't them who cursed her in the first place.

PG. 114 THE FOURTH LABOUR: SCIRON
Because Theseus had persuaded Sciron to turn twice, so he was facing north, which means that Sciron had his back to the cliff and Theseus could easily push him over it.

SOLUTIONS

PG. 116 THE FIFTH LABOUR: KING CERCYON

Because Theseus was still oiled up from his earlier ablutions! Theseus slipped out of the bear-hug hold like a bar of soap; Cercyon could not get another grip, allowing Theseus to then use his superior fighting skills to defeat the mountainous king.

PG. 118 THE FINAL LABOUR: PROCRUSTES THE HOTELIER

He slept in the 3.8m bed, but sideways, so that he fit precisely its 1.9m width.

PG. 119 THE CHALLENGE OF THE PALLANTIDES

Because the two eldest brothers are twins. Therefore, they share the same birthdate; and as Theseus specified only one man could fight him, they would be unable to do so. If they had agreed, the eldest brother could fight; then they would have been able to, as even twins are born in order, which is why Theseus was so careful with his words. (If you guessed triplets, quadruplets or any other multiple births you may also consider this puzzle solved.)

PG. 120 THE TRIBUTES

He was disguised as one of the young women, not the young men.

PG. 121 FINDING THE ENTRANCE

He took every third word of the ladies' sentences, which makes, "You must go east, find three vines and climb."

PG. 122 RIDDLE OF THE MINOTAUR

The brooch pin. If Theseus had answered "the sword," as the Minotaur had perhaps intended, he would have died from the poison. But the brooch pin is also metal and sharp at one end, and made Theseus bleed slightly when pricked with it.

SOLUTIONS

PG. 123 PART I: PENELOPE'S ONE-HUNDRED AND EIGHT SUITORS

25%. 108 divided by 12 is 9. If the second dice roll comes up 10-12, she can have a day off, and there's a 3/12, or one quarter, chance of that happening.

PG. 124 PART II: CALYPSO'S ISLAND

He said he wanted to die. But the question did not specify that Calypso would kill him. Everyone, if not immortal, dies eventually. And so, she let him depart.

PG. 125 PART III: DON'T FORGET THE LOTUS

It had a blue middle and golden petals with vermilion edges. Well done for not cheating.

PG. 126 IV: SLEEPING CYCLOPS

Because the cave entrance is blocked by the boulder, and if they kill him while it is sealed, they won't be able to roll it out of the way and escape.

PG. 128 PART V: OL' ONE EYE IS BACK

The one in front. Polyphemus is staring out of the cave to the east at sunrise, so the sun would be directly in his wounded eye. Attacking from the back or sides would not convey significant advantage because of his senses, but his eye is still the most vulnerable spot.

PG. 129 PART VI: THE OLD WINDBAG

Because the winds lay in the bag as they do on a map, and therefore the north was at the top and escaped when Odysseus peered inside.

PG. 130 PART VII: SIREN SIGNS

Because she was in the eastern part of the beach, right next to the very loud waterfall, and therefore would not be heard even if she did sing.

SOLUTIONS

PG. 132 PART VIII: STEER CLEAR

The herder is actually Poseidon. He sits on a horse, bears a trident-like crook, has a beard like a storm cloud and a rumbling voice like an earthquake, and casts a sea-spray-like mist over the sailors.

PG. 134 PART IX: ODYSSEUS, MASTER OF DISGUISE

Odysseus asked for water from the clean well in the courtyard, but he could not see it past the swineherd's hut, and he claimed he knew nothing about the household.

PG. 136 PART X: ODYSSEUS KILLS THE ONE HUNDRED AND EIGHT SUITORS

He sang the Sirens' song, drawing them irresistibly to him. He learned it from hearing them on the beach, and the notation on the stones indicated to him the truth that the song is not some ability possessed only by them, but is in fact something that can be learned.

PG. 137 PSYCHOPOMP, QU'EST-CE QUE C'EST?

The Cyclopes, because they each only have one eye, and therefore have only one coin to take to Charon.

PG. 138 CROSSING THE RIVER LETHE

Using the gold brooch and a branch from a tree, the Sibyl can mime to him what he needs to do from the right bank while he is on the left; the river is only eight yards wide, so she will be visible.

PG. 140 OUROBOROS

His statement "three and three become six" indicates that if you take the last three words of the puzzle's text and combine it with the first three (like a word snake eating its own tail) you get the phrase "he stabbed him in the heart." That is where ancient Greeks thought human consciousness and intelligence resided.

SOLUTIONS

PG. 142 HERCULES AND CACUS

Because of the hoofprints in the cowpats. As the cattle are standing in a row, if they had genuinely been moving in the direction of their hoofprints they would not have been stepping in their own cowpats.

PG. 144 KNOT A GOOD IDEA

He could pull out the linchpin, thus detaching the yoke from the ox-cart and making the knots loose enough to see their possible solution.

PG. 146 ANDROCLES AND THE LION AND FOUR OTHER GUYS

Because the first slave out wasn't Androcles. Once Septus had swapped with Simonus and Treva, it meant they were both next to Antonius. As he doesn't like Corinthians, he had to swap with Androcles, meaning he was the first out, and the lion didn't know him at all.

PG. 148 TAKING THE PYTHIA

Going to war destroyed the Lydian empire, not the Persian one.

PG. 150 THE SKILLS OF PIRITHOUS

Because he could tell that Pirithous painted the target on after he had fired the arrows. He had chosen a very big tree to increase his chances of hitting it, and had been forced to draw a very large target so that all three arrows would be inside. Furthermore, when Theseus arrived, Pirithous was picking up the bow, not putting it down, and there were flecks of wet red paint on the tree's splinters, suggesting it had only been recently done, and when Theseus checked the arrow shaft, he saw paint there too.

SOLUTIONS

PG. 152 AN ORACLE MIRACLE

The fourth answer: "If you kill me, you will have great success in the future." While the commander seems to think her predictions are worthless, the soldier seems to understand that whatever she says is usually the opposite of what happens. Therefore, none of the other pronouncements hold weight, and the fourth would suggest to him that he'd instead face misfortune and would be better off letting her live.

PG. 154 NOT A WATERTIGHT SOLUTION

The Amazons' boat wasn't sinking as fast as the men's boat because there was less weight in it. The Amazons were smaller and slimmer, there were fewer of them, and their shields were smaller and fewer as well.

PG. 156 ARTEMIS AND ORION

Artemis' item weights:
Helmet: 1.25kg; Sword: 2kg; Shield: 2.5kg; Breastplate: 2kg; Shin guards: 2kg. Total: 9.75kg.

Orion's item weights:
Helmet: 2.5kg; Sword: 3kg; Shield: 1kg; Breastplate: 8kg; Shin guards: 1.25kg. Total: 15.75kg.

Therefore, Orion should pass his sword to Artemis; then it will weigh 12.75kg on both sides.

PG. 158 DEATH ON THE HALIACMON

Megaera, the fury of jealousy. The man on the deck was one of the sons of the queen (the crying lady). He was jealous of her big day and of the golden baklava, so he ate it and stole her crown (order unknown), and Megaera then punished this act of jealousy.

SOLUTIONS

PG. 160 ROMAN WHISPERS

First, he removed the double vowels:
At exit front noon to. At
black moon-gate right stop.
Descend ceiling from lower.
Then changed the words that
could be written as opposites:
At enter back midnight from. At white
sundial left go. Ascend floor to upper.
Which can be reordered as:
At midnight enter from back. Go left
at white sundial. Ascend to upper floor.

PG. 162 BAD VIBRATIONS

Because her supernaturally light-
footed nymph dancing made no
vibrations on the ground as she
danced, so it wasn't scared away.

PG. 164 ORPHEUS PLAYS THE BLUES

"Sadly, our love is broken with it." Each
of the lines shows a changing pattern
in the number of letters in each word:

2 6 4 2 5 4 4 – By viper's
fang my life's been split.

4 2 6 4 2 5 4 – Thus in darker
tomb be hope quit.

3 4 2 6 4 2 5 – She flit to
worlds under my sight.

Therefore, the next line should be
5 3 4 2 6 4 2, which only matches
"Sadly, our love is broken with it."

PG. 166 COOL CATS

Statement 3 – "If Orpheus enters the
Underworld, he will die" – is a lie, as
the first paragraph shows the gods
are with him. Manticores don't like
music but do seem to like Orpheus'
dancing, so the Manticore that cannot
hear is happily dancing along with
him, while the Manticore that can
hear but not see is sitting solemnly.

SOLUTIONS

PG. 168 THE WALK

As a Auloniad nymph, her footsteps are too light to be heard. If Orpheus had heeded Hades' advice and thought back to when she was alive (or looked back at page 162-3), he may have remembered that.

PG. 170 HOW TO GET AHEAD IN MUSIC

Melpomene. While Calliope was Orpheus' mother, she would recognize that it wasn't him, and wouldn't like the glossolalia. The same is true of Euterpe, who preferred lyrical poetry. But Melpomene, often depicted with a the mask of tragedy and a sharp knife, became the muse of tragedy, suggesting the head's songs had a depressive effect on her.

PG. 172 PART I: CENTAURS OF ATTENTION

Down at the loose rocks under the Centaurs' feet. Her arrow could dislodge them, causing an avalanche that would sweep the Centaurs away.

PG. 174 PART II: MURDER SHE BOWED

Atalanta can run faster than the arrow. So once she's fired it, she can run and catch it after it's been through the bullseye but before it strikes Jessica.

PG. 176 PART III: DON'T SPEAK

Door VII (or 7). Atalanta killed a Vrykolakas and two Ichthyocentaurs, spelling VII.

PG. 178 PART IV: BASILISK FAULTY

The left basilisk's sight killed the man. If it is not partially sighted, it must be the one with full sight. Therefore, the other two are the blind and partially sighted basilisks; and since he said he was wrong about them, that means the middle basilisk must be the partially sighted one and the right basilisk the blind one.

SOLUTIONS

PG. 180 PART V: THE THREE GOLDEN APPLES OF APHRODITE

Because no-one can resist picking up the apples – including Hippomenes. So when he threw them down (not far enough away from himself) he immediately sought to pick them up again, depriving himself of any chance to get ahead of Atalanta.

PG. 182 THE SEER OF DODONA

The prophecy was, "Nothing bad will happen to you if you leave this place." However, he did not leave the temple; he tripped and fell on the rubble on his way to the exit, breaking his neck – the "imminent death" the other oracles foresaw.

PG. 184 A PAIR OF KINGS

Pandareus has the same poison and antidote as Tantalus. So he can give the messenger the antidote, and then give him the poison again, giving him six more days to return to Tantalus and receive the antidote again.

PG. 186 MAKING SACRIFICES

Cratinus.

PG. 188 VRYKOLAKAS

The two knocks were on two different front doors! The first was on that of the home next door, but she heard it clearly because of her proximity and the thin walls of her house. The second was on her own front door.

PG. 190 PLUTO DWARFS HADES

7, 8 and 9. If Pluto's hand has more value than the bag, then it cannot include 1 or 2. The only possible combination that leads to the number 4 in the value of the bag and Pluto's hand is that Pluto has 7, 8 and 9, which adds up to 24, and the bag has 1, 2, 5 and 6, which adds up to 14.

SOLUTIONS

PG. 192 ON THE FIDDLE
G major.

PG. 194 THE CURSE OF NEPTUNE
He died of dehydration. It was his fear of Poseidon, and therefore water, that led to his death.

PG. 196 ZEUS VS JUPITER
3 – Lose. Jupiter is Zeus; he did not say he was beyond fear, and he could easily fight Typhon and trick Cronus. But he himself said he could only win. And if he tried to win by losing, then he would paradoxically lose anyway, because he would have won!

PG. 198 ZEUSICAL CHAIRS
50%. No matter what happens, or which seat Zeus takes, at the end the throne left for Dionysus will either be his or Zeus'. If Zeus randomly takes his own throne, every other god sits down normally. If Zeus randomly takes Dionysus' throne, Dionysus will take Zeus' and every other god will sit down normally. If Zeus randomly takes another god's throne, that god will have to choose between Zeus', Dionysus', or some other god. If they choose another god's throne, that god will have the same choice. If any random god takes Zeus' throne, then the rest will sit down normally, and if any random god takes Dionysus' throne, then the rest will sit down normally – except for Dionysus, who will take Zeus'.

PG. 200 NEPTUNE VS POSEIDON
Because most of Poseidon's men would be dead by the time they reached the river. Sailing three days with no provisions, including drinkable water, would mean most would die of dehydration and starvation. But the river-boatmen had access to fresh water in the form of the river, and in a pinch could even eat one of the horses, so there would be more of them alive than Poseidon's men when battle commenced.

SOLUTIONS

PG. 202 THE TALE OF PROMETHEUS

Credit, by claiming to have accomplished feats that were supposedly done by others.

PG. 204 PART I: MR. BUG GOES TO LUNCH

Because the food was poisoned. Venus had hoped Psyche would eat some in her hunger, and die. When the ants had finished, they had tried the food, but as each ant had died after eating each type they had stopped and reluctantly withdrawn.

PG. 206 PART II: FEELING SHEEPISH

There are sharp briars growing on either side of the river, and the golden sheep are known for butting up against anything near them. So it seems likely that there would be some golden wool snared on the briars. Psyche can sneak up near them and extract the wool, just as the reeds hinted.

PG. 208 PART III: EAGLE VS DRAGONS

Because while they could probably defeat the eagle, he is the icon of Jupiter, and the vengeful god would then probably bring his full powers down onto the dragons.

PG. 210 PART IV: GOING TO THE DOGS

One head should receive boxes 1 and 5 (36 Kochliara plus 24 Kochliara = 60, or 1 hēmina.) The second head should receive box 2 (1 hēmina). And the third head should receive boxes 3 and 4 (40 Kochliara plus 20 Kochliara equals 60 Kochliara, or 1 hēmina).

PG. 212 PART V: AMBROSIA COCKTAIL

Styx water: 8
Nectar: 6
Ambrosia: 5
Ichor: 2

SOLUTIONS

PG. 214 END OF THE CENTURY
Zero. 100 x 0 = 0 and 80 x 0 = 0

PG. 216 SPHINX OF THE RIDDLE
Frogspawn and tadpoles. A tadpole begins with no legs but, beginning with the back legs, grows them over the course of its spawning to become a frog. If you solved this, well done. We will meet again.

PG. 218 HANNIBAL CROSSES THE ALPS
41,580. He started with 50,000, which was reduced by 16% (8,000), leaving him 42,000. They were then reinforced by 10% of 42,000 (4,200), giving them 46,200 troops. This was then reduced by 10% (4,620), leaving Hannibal with 41,580 troops.

PG. 220 UNICORNS!
Because the ancient Greeks considered the unicorn a real animal that lived in another country, and therefore did not include it in their myths, but instead in their accounts of the natural world.

PG. 222 PHYLLIS-OPHICAL
Phyllis is Pandora, the first woman, who opened the pyxis and released either cursed evils or gifts. Her casket or pyxis was the original box, containing the one thing left inside it: hope.

PG. 224 TROY, TROY AGAIN
If the person inside the horse was Helen of Troy, the woman that the war was supposedly fought over in the first place.

SOLUTIONS

PG. 226 YOU'LL NEVER OUTFOX THE FOX

Laelaps, the dog that – legend has it – could catch anything it hunted! The two of them running around created an insoluble paradox that meant Zeus had to intervene by turning them both to stone.

PG. 228 CONSTELLATION PRIZE

Gemini: Castor and Pollux.
Canis major and minor: The Teumessian fox and Laelaps the dog.
Sagitta: The arrow that killed the Stymphalian birds, the Nemean lion or the Cyclops.
Draco: Dragons.
Leo: The Nemean lion.
Aquila: Zeus' eagle.
Centaurus: Centaurs.
Auriga: The charioteer of Oenomaus.
Lyra: The harp or lyre of Orpheus.
Carina: A boat's keel – *carina* is Latin for keel.

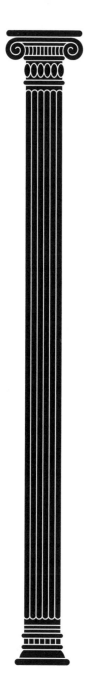

THE END
TO TÉLOS!

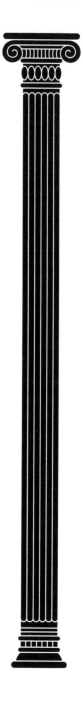